I0334566

IT'S ALWRITE!
A PRACTICAL GUIDE TO WRITING DIFFERENT TEXT TYPES IN ENGLISH

MATT FLETCHER

LORTHEW
— PRESS —

CONTENTS

Preface	v
Introduction	vii
1. Articles (Magazine)	1
2. Blogs	8
3. Brochures & Leaflets	16
4. Cover Letters and Personal Statements	23
5. Diaries & Private Journals	30
6. Emails	36
7. Essays	43
8. Interviews	53
9. Letters	62
10. Letters to the Editor	69
11. News Reports	77
12. Official Reports	85
13. Opinion Columns	93
14. Proposals	100
15. Reviews	110
16. Sets of Instructions & Guidelines	117
17. Social Media Posts	125
18. Speeches	131
About the Author	139

It's Alwrite!: A Practical Guide to Writing Different Text Types in English

Copyright © 2024 Matt Fletcher All rights reserved

No part of this publication may be produced in any form or by any electronic or mechanical means, including information storage and retrieval systems without permission.

For information regarding permission, contact the author at www.matttfletcher.com

For inquiries and details, contact the publisher:

www.lorthewpress.co.uk

Published by Lorthew Press

Paperback ISBN: 978-1-0686692-1-7

eBook ISBN: 978-1-0686692-0-0

PREFACE

For many years, I have had the privilege of teaching the International Baccalaureate (IB) English B course, guiding countless students through the intricate and rewarding journey of mastering English writing. Through this extensive experience, I have observed the common challenges and triumphs that students face when learning to write various text types. This book is a culmination of those years of teaching, learning, and refining the art of writing.

In my classroom, I have always emphasized the importance of understanding the structure, purpose, and audience for each text type. Working closely with students, we have honed templates and strategies that effectively break down these components, making the writing process more approachable and comprehensible. The content within this book represents the distilled wisdom and best practices that have proven successful time and again.

While "It's Alwrite!" is an invaluable resource for IB students and teachers of the English B course, its scope extends far beyond the IB curriculum. This book is designed for anyone eager to deepen their understanding of English text types and improve their writing skills. Whether you are a student, teacher, or an enthusiast of the English

PREFACE

language, you will find detailed guidance on constructing various text types with clarity and precision.

Each chapter provides a comprehensive exploration of a specific text type, including its setting, readership, objective, style, attitude, and standards. Practical tips, useful vocabulary, idiomatic expressions, and a general structure are provided to ensure that you can confidently craft your own texts. Additionally, each section includes an example and layout to illustrate the key points and demonstrate effective writing techniques.

I hope that "It's Alwrite!" serves as a valuable tool in your writing journey, empowering you to express yourself with confidence and skill. May it inspire you to explore the richness of English text types and unlock your full potential as a writer.

Matt Fletcher

INTRODUCTION

English writing is a crucial skill that opens up numerous opportunities in both academic and professional settings. Whether you are crafting an article, composing a letter, writing an email, or creating an advertisement, effective writing can significantly enhance your ability to communicate clearly and persuasively. This book will help you understand the various types of texts you may encounter and provide strategies to improve your writing skills across different contexts.

THE IMPORTANCE OF WRITING IN ENGLISH

Strong writing skills in English are essential for success in a globalized world. They enable you to convey your ideas effectively, engage with diverse audiences, and express yourself with clarity and precision. Good writing not only enhances your communication but also boosts your confidence in various contexts, whether you're engaging in professional correspondence or personal interactions.

This book is designed to be your comprehensive guide to mastering a variety of text types in the English language. Each chapter will delve into a specific form of writing, offering detailed insights and practical tips to help you develop and refine your skills. By the end of this

INTRODUCTION

guide, you will be equipped with the tools and knowledge needed to approach any writing task with confidence.

WHY ENGLISH WRITING MATTERS

English writing is more than just a tool for communication; it's a gateway to expressing your thoughts, sharing your ideas, and connecting with others on a deeper level. Whether you are writing a heartfelt letter to a friend, drafting a critical business proposal, or penning a captivating story, the ability to write well in English can open doors you never imagined.

THE POWER OF THE WRITTEN WORD

The written word has a unique power. It can inform, persuade, entertain, and inspire. Think about the last time you read a book that you couldn't put down or an article that changed your perspective on an important issue. The ability to write effectively allows you to harness this power, making your words resonate with readers and leave a lasting impact.

BUILDING BLOCKS OF EFFECTIVE WRITING:

At the heart of good writing are the fundamental elements that bring your ideas to life: clarity, coherence, and creativity. Clarity ensures your message is understood without ambiguity. Coherence makes your writing logical and easy to follow. Creativity adds a spark that captures the reader's imagination. Mastering these elements will transform your writing from mundane to compelling.

Clarity

Clear writing avoids confusion and misinterpretation. It involves choosing the right words, constructing simple yet powerful sentences, and eliminating unnecessary jargon. Clear writing ensures that your audience understands your message quickly and accurately, which is crucial in both personal and professional contexts.

Coherence

Coherent writing is logical and well-organized. It involves structuring your thoughts in a way that makes sense and flows naturally from one idea to the next. This is achieved through the use of paragraphs, headings, and transitional phrases that guide the reader through your narrative or argument effortlessly.

Creativity

Creative writing captivates and engages the reader. It involves using vivid descriptions, engaging narratives, and imaginative ideas to bring your writing to life. Whether you're writing fiction or non-fiction, creativity adds depth and interest, making your work stand out and resonate with readers.

ADAPTING YOUR WRITING STYLE

Different situations require different writing styles. The ability to adapt your writing style to suit various contexts is a valuable skill. For example, a formal report requires a professional tone and precise language, while a blog post can be more conversational and relaxed. Understanding the nuances of different writing styles and when to use them will enhance your versatility as a writer.

Formal Writing

Formal writing is used in professional and academic settings. It involves a respectful tone, precise vocabulary, and adherence to specific formats and conventions. Examples include business reports, academic essays, and official correspondence. Mastering formal writing is essential for success in many careers and academic pursuits.

Informal Writing

Informal writing is more relaxed and personal. It allows for a conversational tone, colloquial language, and a more flexible structure. Examples include personal letters, emails to friends, and social media posts. Informal writing is ideal for building connections and expressing your personality.

INTRODUCTION

Persuasive Writing

Persuasive writing aims to convince the reader to accept a particular point of view or take a specific action. It involves presenting arguments, using emotional appeals, and supporting your claims with evidence. Examples include opinion articles, advertisements, and political speeches. Persuasive writing is a powerful tool for influencing others and driving change.

Descriptive Writing

Descriptive writing paints a vivid picture for the reader. It uses sensory details and figurative language to create a rich and immersive experience. Examples include travel writing, descriptive essays, and creative fiction. Descriptive writing engages the reader's senses and emotions, making your work memorable.

Narrative Writing

Narrative writing tells a story. It involves creating characters, setting scenes, and developing plots that captivate the reader's imagination. Examples include novels, short stories, and memoirs. Narrative writing is a fundamental skill for any writer looking to entertain and engage their audience.

Expository Writing

Expository writing explains or informs. It involves presenting facts, providing explanations, and offering insights in a clear and straightforward manner. Examples include instructional manuals, research papers, and news articles. Expository writing is essential for educating and informing your readers.

GETTING STARTED:

The journey to becoming a skilled writer begins with practice and dedication. Here are some tips to help you get started:

- **Read Widely:** Expose yourself to different genres and styles of writing. Pay attention to how authors structure

their work, develop their ideas, and use language effectively.
- **Write Regularly:** Make writing a daily habit. Set aside time each day to write, whether it's a journal entry, a blog post, or a short story.
- **Seek Feedback:** Share your writing with others and be open to constructive criticism. Feedback from peers, teachers, or mentors can provide valuable insights and help you improve.
- **Revise and Edit:** Writing is a process that involves multiple drafts. Don't be afraid to revise and edit your work until it's polished and refined.
- **Experiment:** Try writing in different styles and genres. Experimenting with various forms of writing will help you discover your strengths and interests.

THE TEXT TYPES:

In this book we will cover the following text types:

- Article (Magazine)
- Blogs
- Brochure/Leaflet
- Cover Letter and Personal Statement
- Diary/Private Journal
- Email
- Essay
- Interviews
- Letter
- Letter to the Editor
- News Reports
- Official Report
- Opinion Column
- Proposal
- Review
- Set of Instructions & Guidelines
- Social Media Post

INTRODUCTION

- Speech

THE ROAD AHEAD

This book is your roadmap to mastering English writing. Each chapter will explore a different type of writing text type, offering practical tips, examples, and practice exercises to help you develop your skills. Whether you're looking to excel in academic writing, enhance your professional communication, or simply enjoy the creative process, this book will provide the tools and knowledge you need to succeed.

With practice and perseverance, you'll become a confident and versatile writer, capable of tackling any writing challenge that comes your way. Let's dive in and start mastering the art of English writing!

CHAPTER 1
ARTICLES (MAGAZINE)

A MAGAZINE ARTICLE is a piece of writing published in a periodical, typically designed to inform, entertain, or persuade readers. Unlike news articles, which are brief and focused on current events, magazine articles often explore topics in greater depth and detail. They can cover a wide range of subjects, including lifestyle, culture, politics, health, technology, and more.

Magazine articles are characterized by their engaging style and well-researched content, often incorporating interviews, expert opinions, and personal anecdotes. They aim to capture the reader's interest from the first sentence, providing a compelling narrative that is both informative and enjoyable to read. Whether you're flipping through the pages of a glossy fashion magazine or reading an in-depth feature in a news journal, magazine articles offer a rich and varied reading experience that goes beyond the surface of the topic at hand.

SETTING, READERSHIP, OBJECTIVE:

- The setting for an article can vary depending on the publication and the specific section it's featured in. It could be a news article reporting on current events, a feature article

delving into a particular topic or issue, or an opinion piece expressing the author's viewpoint on a relevant subject.
- The readership of an article also varies based on the publication's target audience. It could be a general audience interested in staying informed about local or global news, or a niche audience seeking specialized knowledge or insights.
- The objective of an article is typically to inform, educate, entertain, or persuade the readership. It may aim to provide factual information, analyze a complex issue, tell a compelling story, or advocate for a particular stance or solution.

STYLE AND ATTITUDE:

- Adopts a formal and authoritative style appropriate for the publication and audience.
- The tone can vary depending on the type of article but is generally objective and impartial, presenting facts and arguments in a balanced manner.
- Maintains a professional demeanor while still engaging the reader's interest and attention.

STANDARDS:

- Typically written in the third person to maintain objectivity and credibility.
- Includes a headline or title that accurately summarizes the article's content and grabs the reader's attention.
- Follows a clear and logical structure, with an introduction that hooks the reader, body paragraphs that provide supporting evidence or arguments, and a conclusion that reinforces the main points or offers a final thought.
- Cites sources and provides evidence to support claims or assertions, maintaining journalistic integrity and credibility.

TIPS AND TEMPLATES:

Writing an article for a newspaper or magazine provides an opportunity to inform, educate, or entertain a wide audience. It's important to maintain a professional tone and adhere to journalistic standards while still engaging the reader's interest. Consider the publication's audience and editorial guidelines when crafting your article, and strive to provide valuable insights or information that will resonate with readers.

- **Useful Vocabulary:** Using precise and descriptive language is essential for conveying information effectively in an article. For example, instead of saying "good," you could use "commendable" or "exemplary." Additionally, incorporating industry-specific terminology or jargon can demonstrate your expertise and enhance the article's credibility.
- **Idiomatic Expressions:** While idiomatic expressions are less common in formal writing such as articles, incorporating figurative language or vivid imagery can still enhance the reader's understanding and engagement. For instance, instead of saying "important," you could use "a key player" or "a driving force." Use idioms sparingly and only when they add depth or nuance to your writing, being mindful of the publication's style and tone guidelines.

ARTICLES (MAGAZINE)

TITLE HERE
Author Name | Date of Publication

Image with caption

Introduction:
Hook the Reader: Start with an engaging opening sentence or question.
Provide Background Information: Offer some context or background on the topic.
State the Main Point: Clearly outline the purpose or main idea of the article.

First Main Point:
Explanation: Describe the first main idea or argument.
Support: Provide evidence, examples, or quotes to support this point.

Second Main Point:
Explanation: Describe the second main idea or argument.
Support: Provide evidence, examples, or quotes to support this point.

Third Main Point:
Explanation: Describe the third main idea or argument.
Support: Provide evidence, examples, or quotes to support this point.

Conclusion
Summarize Key Points: Recap the main ideas discussed in the article.
Restate the Main Message: Reinforce the purpose or takeaway of the article.
Closing Thought: End with a memorable statement or quote.

Call to Action or Next Steps
Engage the Reader: Encourage the reader to take action, think further, or seek more information.
Provide Resources: Suggest books, websites, or other articles for further reading.

Sources/Citations
Cite References: List any sources or references used to support the article's content.
Provide Credibility: Ensure that all information is accurately attributed to maintain the article's credibility.

Article layout template

ARTICLE EXAMPLE:

Rocking the Charts: Meet The Electric Vibe, London's Hottest New Band
By Peter Finch | May 22, 2024
Rockzine Forever

London's music scene has a new sensation that's causing quite a stir. The Electric Vibe, a dynamic rock band, has taken the city by storm with their electrifying performances and unforgettable sound. Fans and critics alike are buzzing about this up-and-coming group that's set to redefine rock music.

Who Are The Electric Vibe?

The Electric Vibe consists of four talented musicians: lead vocalist Alex T, guitarist Jase, bassist Brooks, and drummer Chlo. Formed just two years ago, the band quickly gained a loyal following in London's underground music scene. Their unique blend of classic rock riffs and modern melodies has captivated audiences, making them a standout act.

The Breakthrough Moment

Their big break came earlier this year when they performed at the legendary Roundhouse. The sold-out show was a turning point, and their performance left the crowd in awe. "The energy was through the roof," said one fan. "I've never seen anything like it." The band's charismatic stage presence and powerful music created an unforgettable experience.

What Sets Them Apart?

What makes The Electric Vibe so special? It's their ability to connect with the audience. Their lyrics, often reflecting personal experiences and social issues, resonate deeply with fans. Jase's guitar solos are nothing short of mesmerizing, while Alex T's raw and powerful vocals

ARTICLES (MAGAZINE)

bring an emotional intensity to their songs. As one critic put it, "They play as if their lives depend on it, and it shows."

Upcoming Album and Tour

The band's much-anticipated debut album, "Voltage," is set to release next month. The first single, "High Voltage," has already topped the charts, and fans can't get enough. To support the album, The Electric Vibe will embark on a nationwide tour, hitting major cities across the UK.

What's Next?

With their star on the rise, The Electric Vibe is on the brink of stardom. Music insiders are predicting big things for this talented group. As Alex T aptly put it in a recent interview, "We're just getting started. The best is yet to come."

So, if you haven't heard of The Electric Vibe yet, it's time to tune in. Their music is more than just a sound; it's a movement that's ready to take the world by storm. Catch them live on December 21st at The T Club, London, and you'll understand why everyone is talking about London's hottest new band.

PRACTICE TASKS:

Question 1:

You have been asked to write an article for a travel magazine that you subscribe to. Write an article that describes a recent trip you took to an exotic location, informs readers about the cultural highlights of the destination, and provides practical tips for travelers planning a similar journey.

Question 2:

You have been asked to write an article for a health and wellness magazine that you subscribe to. Write an article that describes the benefits of a plant-based diet, informs readers about the nutritional aspects of plant-based foods, and offers practical advice on how to transition to this type of diet.

CHAPTER 2
BLOGS

A BLOG IS an online platform where individuals or organizations regularly publish content on a wide variety of topics. Blogs are typically informal and conversational in tone, making them a popular medium for sharing personal stories, opinions, and expertise. Unlike traditional articles, blog posts often include multimedia elements such as images, videos, and hyperlinks to enhance the reader's experience.

Blogging allows writers to connect with a global audience, fostering interaction and community through comments and social media sharing. Whether you're chronicling your travel adventures, offering tips on a hobby, or providing insights into your professional field, blogs are a versatile and dynamic way to engage with readers and share valuable information.

SETTING, READERSHIP, OBJECTIVE:

- The setting for a blog post can vary widely, depending on the niche or topic of the blog. It could be a personal blog where the writer shares experiences from their life, a professional blog offering advice or insights in a particular field, or even a niche blog focusing on a specific hobby or interest.

- The readership of a blog post can also be diverse, ranging from friends and family to a wider online audience interested in the blog's topic. Understanding the target audience is crucial for tailoring the content and tone of the post.
- The objective of a blog post is typically to inform, entertain, persuade, or engage the audience. It may aim to share personal experiences, provide valuable information or opinions, spark discussion, or promote a product or service.

STYLE AND ATTITUDE:

- Adopts a conversational and engaging style, similar to talking to a friend or colleague.
- The tone can vary depending on the topic and intended audience but is generally informal and approachable.
- Allows for creativity and personality to shine through, making the post unique to the author's voice.

STANDARDS:

- Often written in the first person but can also be written in the third person or from multiple perspectives, depending on the blog's style and preferences.
- Includes a headline or title that grabs the reader's attention and summarizes the post's content.
- Incorporates multimedia elements such as images, videos, or infographics to enhance the post's visual appeal and engage the audience.
- Encourages reader interaction through comments, likes, and shares, fostering a sense of community around the blog.

TIPS AND TEMPLATES:

A blog post is an excellent platform for expressing your thoughts, sharing experiences, and connecting with others who share similar

BLOGS

interests. Keep your writing authentic and relatable, and don't be afraid to inject your personality into your posts. Remember to consider your audience and tailor your content to meet their needs and expectations.

- **Useful Vocabulary:** Incorporating vivid and descriptive language can make your blog posts more engaging. Consider using words that evoke imagery and emotions, such as "breathtaking," "captivating," or "heartwarming." Additionally, using industry-specific terminology or jargon can demonstrate your expertise and credibility in a particular subject area.
- **Idiomatic Expressions:** Including idiomatic expressions can add flair and personality to your writing, making it more memorable for readers. For example, instead of saying "I'm excited about," you could use "I'm over the moon about," or instead of "I have a lot of work to do," you could say "I have my work cut out for me." Just be mindful of your audience and ensure that the idioms you use are appropriate and easily understood.

IT'S ALWRITE!

BLOG TITLE HERE

Author Name | Date of Publication | Website | Tags | Categories

Introduction:

Engage the Reader: Start with a personal anecdote, interesting fact, or a provocative question.
Introduce the Topic: Provide some background or context for the post.
State the Purpose: Clearly outline what the reader can expect to learn or gain from the post.

First Main Point

Description: Encourage the reader to take action, think further, or seek more information.
Support: Provide examples, personal experiences, or data to support this point.

[Image with caption]

Second Main Point

Description: Explain the second key idea or piece of information.
Support: Provide examples, personal experiences, or data to support this point.

[Image with caption]

Third Main Point

Description: Explain the third key idea or piece of information.
Support: Provide examples, personal experiences, or data to support this point.

Conclusion/Summarise Key Points

Summarize Key Points: Recap the main ideas discussed in the post.
Reinforce the Message: Restate the main takeaway or lesson.
Encourage Engagement: Invite readers to comment, share their thoughts, or ask questions.

Call to Action

Engage Further: Encourage the reader to take a specific action, such as subscribing to the blog, following on social media, or downloading a resource.
Provide Next Steps: Suggest related blog posts or resources for further reading.

Blog Template

BLOGS

BLOG EXAMPLE

Exploring London: A Memorable Adventure
By Emily Johnson | August 22, 2022
www.travellingtheworldwithEJ.internet

London, the vibrant capital of the United Kingdom, has always been on my travel bucket list. This past week, I finally had the chance to explore its historic streets, iconic landmarks, and diverse culture. Here's a glimpse into my unforgettable adventure in this bustling metropolis.

Day 1: Arrival and First Impressions

Landing at Heathrow Airport, I was immediately struck by the city's energy. The journey to our hotel in Covent Garden was smooth, thanks to the efficient London Underground. After checking in, my friend Sarah and I decided to explore our surroundings.

Covent Garden and The West End

Covent Garden was buzzing with activity. Street performers, market stalls, and the aroma of delicious food filled the air. We grabbed lunch at a charming café, where we enjoyed some traditional British fare. The fish and chips were crispy and satisfying.

In the evening, we caught a show in the West End. Watching a live performance in one of London's historic theatres was a dream come true. The production was breathtaking, and the atmosphere was electric.

Day 2: Iconic Landmarks

Our second day was dedicated to sightseeing. We started with a visit to the Tower of London. The Beefeaters' tales of history and intrigue were fascinating.

Next, we walked across Tower Bridge, marvelling at the engineering feat. From there, we made our way to the British Museum. The vast collection of artefacts from around the world was overwhelming.

Afternoon Tea at The Ritz

A trip to London wouldn't be complete without experiencing afternoon tea. We booked a reservation at The Ritz and indulged in an elegant afternoon of tea, scones, and delicate pastries. The opulence of the setting made us feel like royalty.

Day 3: Parks and Palaces

On our third day, we decided to take it easy and enjoy London's beautiful green spaces. We strolled through Hyde Park, where we rented bicycles and rode around the Serpentine. The tranquility of the park was a welcome respite from the city's hustle and bustle.

Later, we visited Buckingham Palace. While we didn't see the Queen, the Changing of the Guard ceremony was a sight to behold. One of the locals standing next to us said, "Blimey, those guards don't bat an eyelid!" Sarah looked puzzled and whispered to me, "What does 'blimey' mean?" I explained it was a British expression of surprise.

Evening at Camden Market

We spent our final evening exploring Camden Market. The eclectic mix of stalls, street food, and live music made for a vibrant atmosphere. We sampled international cuisines and shopped for unique souvenirs. While browsing, a vendor told us, "These trinkets are selling like hotcakes!" Sarah was confused again and asked me, "What are hotcakes?" I laughed and explained it means the items were selling very quickly.

Reflections

Our trip to London was everything we had hoped for and more. From its historic landmarks to its modern attractions, the city offered a perfect blend of the old and the new. As we boarded our flight home, I couldn't help but feel grateful for the memories we made and the experiences we shared.

BLOGS

If you're planning a trip to London, my advice is simple: embrace the adventure and explore off the beaten path. London has something for everyone, and I can't wait to return someday.

Let me know some of your favourite places in the U.K. in the comments below!
See you in the next post!

PRACTICE TASKS

Question 1:

You have been asked to write a blog post for a popular travel blog. Write a blog post that describes a hidden gem in your hometown, informs readers about its history and significance, and provides practical tips for visitors looking to explore this location.

Question 2:

You have been asked to write a blog post for a fitness and wellness blog. Write a blog post that describes your journey to achieving a fitness goal, informs readers about the strategies and exercises that worked for you, and offers motivational tips for others pursuing similar goals.

CHAPTER 3
BROCHURES & LEAFLETS

A BROCHURE or leaflet is a printed document used primarily for promotional or informational purposes in various settings such as businesses, events, or organizations. These materials are designed to be visually appealing and concise, providing key information in an easily digestible format. Whether you're showcasing products, promoting an event, or informing a community about an initiative, brochures and leaflets are effective tools for communication.

While the terms brochure and leaflet are often used interchangeably, they do have distinct differences:

- **Brochure:** Typically more detailed and visually appealing, brochures often include multiple pages or panels, usually folded into bi-fold (two panels) or tri-fold (three panels) formats. They are generally used for promotional purposes, providing comprehensive information about products or services in settings like trade shows, product packages, or point-of-sale locations.
- **Leaflet:** Usually a single sheet of paper, printed on one or both sides, leaflets are less elaborate than brochures and are designed for quick consumption. They are often used for advertising or providing simple information, such as

announcements or general awareness campaigns, and are commonly distributed en masse by handing out on the street, leaving in public places, or door-to-door distribution.

SETTING, READERSHIP, OBJECTIVE:

- Brochures and leaflets are typically used for promotional or informational purposes in various settings such as businesses, events, or organizations.
- The readership of a brochure/leaflet can vary depending on its distribution method and target audience. It could be aimed at potential customers, event attendees, or members of a specific community.
- The objective of a brochure/leaflet is usually to provide concise and visually appealing information that informs, persuades, or encourages action. It may aim to showcase products or services, promote an event or cause, or provide important information about an organization or initiative.

STYLE AND ATTITUDE:

- Adopts a visually appealing layout with attention-grabbing design elements such as colors, images, and typography.
- The tone is typically friendly, informative, and persuasive, aiming to engage the reader and encourage them to take action.
- Allows for clear and concise messaging, focusing on key points and benefits to the reader.

STANDARDS:

- Utilizes a well-organized layout with sections for different topics such as introduction, features/benefits, testimonials, contact information, etc.

- Includes eye-catching visuals such as photographs, illustrations, or graphics to complement the text and enhance readability.
- Incorporates persuasive language and calls to action (CTAs) to prompt the reader to take the desired action, such as making a purchase, attending an event, or contacting the organization.

TIPS AND TEMPLATES:

Designing an effective brochure/leaflet requires careful consideration of both visual appeal and informative content. Keep your messaging clear and concise, focusing on the benefits to the reader. Use compelling visuals and persuasive language to engage your audience and encourage them to take action.

USEFUL VOCABULARY:

Choose words that are clear, descriptive, and easy to understand. Highlight the key features and benefits of your products or services using persuasive language. For example, instead of saying "good quality," you could use "premium" or "high-end."

IDIOMATIC EXPRESSIONS:

While idiomatic expressions may be less common in brochure/leaflet content, you can still use language that resonates with your target audience. Focus on conveying your message in a straightforward and engaging manner, avoiding overly complex or abstract language. For instance, instead of saying "cutting-edge technology," you could use "state-of-the-art" or "advanced."

IT'S ALWRITE!

CATCHY HEADLINE/TITLE

Introduction:
Brief overview of offerings

Features/Benefits:
Bullet points or short paragraphs

Testimonials
Quotes or Reviews from satisfied customers

Call to Action
Encouragement to contact or visit

Contact Information
Address, phone numbers, website, social media etc.

Back cover if needed or below
• Additional information or secondary call to action
• Closing statement or tagline

Leaflet Template

BROCHURES & LEAFLETS

LEAFLET EXAMPLE

Downtown Sing-Off
Unleash Your Inner Star at the Ultimate Singing Competition!

Date: June 15, 2022
Time: 3:00 PM - 8:00 PM
Location: Central Plaza, Downtown
About the Event:
Join us for the most exciting singing competition of the year! Whether you're a shower singer or a seasoned performer, the Downtown Sing-Off is your chance to shine. Show off your vocal talents, compete for amazing prizes, and enjoy a day of music and fun.

How to Enter:
Registration: Open from May 1 - June 10
Entry Fee: $10 per participant

Categories:
Solo Performance
Group Performance (up to 5 members)
Youth Performance (under 18)

To register, visit our website at www.downtownsingoff.com or sign up in person at the Downtown Community Center.

Prizes:
1st Place: $500 cash prize + Recording Session
2nd Place: $300 cash prize
3rd Place: $200 cash prize
Audience Choice Award: $100 cash prize

Event Highlights:
Live performances by local bands and artists
Food trucks and vendors
Fun activities for all ages
Special guest judges from the music industry

Important Information:
Sound Check: Begins at 1:00 PM

Performance Order: Announced on June 12 via our website
Audience: Open to all! Bring your friends and family for an unforgettable day of music.

Contact Us:
For more information, visit our website or contact us at info@downtownsingoff.com or (123) 456-7890.

Follow us on social media for updates and announcements

Don't miss your chance to be the next big star!
Central Plaza, Downtown | June 15, 2024 | 3:00 PM - 8:00 PM

PRACTICE TASKS

Task 1:

You have been asked to create a brochure for a local tourism board. Write a brochure that describes the top attractions in your city, informs visitors about the cultural and historical significance of these sites, and provides practical information such as opening hours, ticket prices, and contact details. Include engaging visuals and a call to action encouraging readers to visit your city.

Task 2:

You have been asked to design a leaflet for a health and wellness fair. Write a leaflet that describes the key events and workshops at the fair, informs attendees about the benefits of participating in these activities, and provides logistical information such as the schedule, location, and registration details. Use persuasive language to encourage attendance and include testimonials from previous participants to highlight the fair's impact.

CHAPTER 4
COVER LETTERS AND PERSONAL STATEMENTS

PERSONAL STATEMENTS and cover letters are essential documents used in academic and professional settings to introduce oneself, highlight qualifications, and express interest in a particular opportunity or position. These documents serve as a critical first impression, showcasing the applicant's unique experiences, skills, and motivations. Whether you're applying for a job, an internship, a scholarship, or a place in a competitive academic program, a well-crafted personal statement or cover letter can make all the difference. They allow you to go beyond the basic facts and figures of your resume or application form, giving you the chance to tell your story, explain why you're passionate about the field, and demonstrate how your background makes you an ideal candidate. In essence, personal statements and cover letters are your opportunity to make a compelling case for yourself, capturing the reader's attention and persuading them to move your application to the next stage.

SETTING, READERSHIP, OBJECTIVE:

- Personal statements and cover letters are typically used in the contexts of college applications, job applications, internships,

scholarships, and other professional or academic opportunities.
- The readership for these documents includes admissions committees, hiring managers, recruiters, or any individuals responsible for selecting candidates for educational programs or job positions.
- The objective of a personal statement or cover letter is to present oneself in a compelling and positive light, demonstrating relevant qualifications and enthusiasm for the opportunity. They aim to persuade the reader that the applicant is a strong fit for the role or program and stands out among other candidates.

STYLE AND ATTITUDE:

- Personal statements and cover letters adopt a formal yet personable style. They balance professionalism with a touch of individuality, reflecting the applicant's personality and passion.
- The tone is confident, positive, and enthusiastic. These documents should convey the applicant's genuine interest in the opportunity and highlight their strengths and achievements without appearing boastful.

STANDARDS

- **Introduction**: Begins with a strong opening statement that captures the reader's attention and provides a brief overview of the applicant's background and purpose.
- **Body Paragraphs**: Detailed sections that highlight key experiences, skills, and accomplishments relevant to the opportunity. These paragraphs should provide specific examples and evidence to support the applicant's claims.
- **Conclusion**: Summarizes the main points, reiterates interest in the opportunity, and includes a call to action, such as

requesting an interview or expressing willingness to provide further information.
- **Customization**: Tailors the content to the specific opportunity, addressing the needs and preferences of the reader. This involves researching the organization or institution to align the document with their values and goals.

TIPS AND TEMPLATES

- **Clarity and Conciseness**: Keep your writing clear and concise. Avoid unnecessary jargon or complex language. Focus on presenting your qualifications and motivations in a straightforward manner.
- **Specificity**: Use specific examples and experiences to illustrate your points. This makes your document more engaging and credible.
- **Customization**: Customize each personal statement or cover letter for the specific opportunity. Highlight how your background and skills make you a perfect fit for the role or program.
- **Professionalism**: Maintain a professional tone throughout the document. Proofread carefully to avoid any grammatical or typographical errors.
- **Enthusiasm**: Show genuine enthusiasm for the opportunity. Your passion and interest should come through in your writing, making you a memorable candidate.

COVER LETTERS AND PERSONAL STATEMENTS

Senders Address:
Name
Address
City, State, Zip Code
Email Address
Phone Number
Date

Recipient's Address:
Name
Title
Company Name
Address
City, State, Zip Code

Salutation:
Dear (Recipient's Name)

Introduction Paragraph:
Opening Statement: A strong opening sentence that captures the reader's interest.
Purpose: Clearly state the position you are applying for and where you found the job listing.
Brief Overview: Provide a brief overview of your background and why you are interested in the position.

First Paragraph:
Key Qualification/Experience: Highlight a key qualification or experience relevant to the position.
Example/Evidence: Provide specific examples and evidence to support your claim.
Impact: Explain the impact or results of your experience or skill.

Second Paragraph:
Key Qualification/Experience: Highlight a key qualification or experience relevant to the position.
Example/Evidence: Provide specific examples and evidence to support your claim.
Impact: Explain the impact or results of your experience or skill.

Third Paragraph:
Key Qualification/Experience: Highlight a key qualification or experience relevant to the position.
Example/Evidence: Provide specific examples and evidence to support your claim.
Impact: Explain the impact or results of your experience or skill.

Concluding Paragraph
Summary of Qualifications: Summarize your key qualifications and experiences.
Restate Interest and Fit: Reiterate your interest in the position and explain why you are a good fit.
Call to Action: Mention your desire for an interview and provide your contact information.

Closing
Sincerely/Best regards/Kind regards,
[Your Name]

Cover Letter Template

EXAMPLE OF COVER LETTER

JD McClaren

123 Main Street

Downtown, USA, 11111

JD.Mcclaren@coolmail.net

555-555-5555

May 22, 2024

Mr. John Smith

Hiring Manager

Tech Innovators Inc.

456 Corporate Avenue

Downtown, USA, 22222

Dear Mr. Smith,

I am writing to express my interest in the Software Developer position at Tech Innovators Inc. as advertised on your company website. With a Bachelor's degree in Computer Science, over three years of professional experience in software development, and a strong passion for innovative technology solutions, I am excited about the opportunity to contribute to your team.

During my tenure at ABC Technologies, I have developed and implemented numerous software solutions that have significantly enhanced the company's operational efficiency. One of my most notable achievements was leading a team to design and deploy a customer relationship management system that improved client interaction tracking by 40%. My role involved full-stack development, from gathering requirements and designing the architecture to coding and testing the final product. This experience honed my skills in various programming languages, including Java, Python, and JavaScript, and strengthened my ability to work collaboratively in a fast-paced environment.

In addition to my technical expertise, I am particularly drawn to Tech Innovators Inc. due to your commitment to pioneering advancements in artificial intelligence and machine learning. I am eager to bring my background in these areas, including a recent project where I integrated machine learning algorithms to enhance predictive analytics for a financial services firm. The project reduced processing time by 25% and provided more accurate forecasting models.

Furthermore, I am impressed by your company's culture of continuous learning and innovation. I am confident that my proactive approach and eagerness to stay at the forefront of technological advancements align well with your team's goals. I am enthusiastic about the possibility of contributing to cutting-edge projects and collaborating with a talented group of professionals.

Thank you for considering my application. I look forward to the opportunity to discuss how my background, skills, and enthusiasms can contribute to the continued success of Tech Innovators Inc. I am available at your earliest convenience for an interview and can be reached at 555-555-5555 or JD.Mcclaren@coolmail.net.

Sincerely,

JD McClaren

PRACTICE TASKS

Task 1:

You are applying for a Marketing Manager position at a well-known digital marketing agency. Write a cover letter that highlights your experience in digital marketing, your successful campaigns, and your ability to lead a team. Make sure to tailor your letter to the specific needs of the agency, demonstrating your knowledge of their work and how you can contribute to their success.

Task 2:

You are applying for a graduate program in Environmental Science at a prestigious university. Write a personal statement that discusses your academic background, research interests, and career goals. Explain why you are passionate about environmental science and how the program aligns with your aspirations.

CHAPTER 5
DIARIES & PRIVATE JOURNALS

A DIARY or private journal is a personal document used to record thoughts, feelings, and experiences on a regular basis. Unlike other forms of writing, diaries and journals are typically intended for the writer's eyes only, serving as a safe space for self-reflection and emotional expression. They provide an opportunity to chronicle daily events, explore inner thoughts, and track personal growth over time.

Diaries and journals are unique in their informality and intimacy. The writing style is often candid and spontaneous, reflecting the writer's authentic voice. Entries can vary in length and depth, ranging from brief notes about daily occurrences to detailed reflections on significant events. This form of writing encourages honesty and creativity, allowing individuals to explore their emotions, set goals, and gain insights into their lives.

SETTING, READERSHIP, OBJECTIVE:

- Diaries and private journals are personal documents used for recording thoughts, feelings, and experiences.
- The readership of a diary/private journal is typically limited to

- the author themselves, although it may also be shared with a trusted confidant or kept for posterity.
- The objective of a diary/private journal is to serve as a private space for self-reflection, emotional expression, and personal growth. It may also serve as a record of significant events or experiences in the author's life.

STYLE AND ATTITUDE:

- Adopts an informal and intimate style, as if writing to oneself or a close friend.
- The tone is personal, honest, and reflective, allowing the author to explore their inner thoughts and emotions freely.
- Allows for spontaneity and authenticity, with no pressure to conform to external standards or expectations.

STANDARDS:

- Typically written in the first person, addressing the author directly or using personal pronouns such as "I" and "me."
- May include dates or timestamps to provide context for entries and track the passage of time.
- Encourages free-flowing writing without worrying about grammar, spelling, or punctuation, focusing instead on capturing raw thoughts and emotions.

TIPS AND TEMPLATES

Keeping a diary or private journal can be a valuable tool for self-discovery, self-expression, and personal growth. Write honestly and authentically, allowing yourself to explore your innermost thoughts and feelings without judgment. Remember that this is your private space, so feel free to be as open and candid as you wish.

- **Useful Vocabulary** Use words that accurately capture your thoughts and emotions, allowing you to express yourself effectively. Consider using descriptive language to evoke imagery and emotions, creating a vivid picture of your experiences. For example, instead of saying "sad," you could use "heartbroken" or "devastated."
- **Idiomatic Expressions:** Incorporating idiomatic expressions can add depth and nuance to your writing, allowing you to convey complex emotions or experiences more effectively. Draw on idioms that resonate with you personally, using them to enhance the richness and authenticity of your journal entries. For instance, instead of saying "I feel overwhelmed," you could use "I'm drowning in a sea of emotions."

IT'S ALWRITE!

Date/Time Stamp Here

Opening:
Dear Diary

Body Paragraph (Free flowing thoughts and emotions)

Daily Events: Describe the day's events or activities, highlighting any significant moments.
Feelings and Reflections: Express your feelings about the events and reflect on their impact.
Personal Insights: Note any personal insights or realizations that arise during the writing process.

Closing Remarks or Reflections

Summary: Summarize the key points or emotions of the entry.
Future Outlook: Consider any plans, hopes, or goals for the future.

Optional throughout:
Sketches, doodles, ideas

Closing
Goodnight, Diary

Diary Template

DIARY EXAMPLE

May 22, 2024

Dear Diary,

Today, the rain poured down on our holiday in Lakeview. I woke up to the sound of raindrops tapping against the window, feeling a bit disappointed since I had planned to explore the local trails. Instead, I decided to make the most of our day indoors.

After a cozy breakfast at our bed and breakfast, we spent the morning by the fireplace. I curled up with "The Secret Garden" and lost myself in its pages while the rain continued outside. The warmth of the fire and the quiet of the inn made for a perfect reading spot.

In the afternoon, we ventured out in our raincoats to a nearby café, "Rainy Day Retreat." Despite getting drenched, the café's atmosphere was delightful, with local art on the walls and the smell of fresh coffee. We enjoyed hot chocolate and sandwiches while watching the rain-soaked streets and playing board games. It was the perfect way to make lemonade out of lemons.

Returning to the inn for dinner, we had a delicious stew prepared by Mrs. Harris, the innkeeper. The evening was spent playing charades with other guests, filling the room with laughter.

Although we didn't explore the outdoors, the day turned out wonderfully. The rain brought a sense of relaxation and connection, making it a memorable part of our holiday. As I drift off to sleep, the gentle drizzle outside is a comforting end to a surprisingly lovely day.

Goodnight, Diary.

Violet

PRACTICE TASKS

Task 1:

You have just returned from a memorable trip to a new city. Write a diary entry that captures the events of the day, describes the places you visited, and reflects on how these experiences made you feel. Be sure to include details about your interactions with people, the sights and sounds of the city, and any personal insights or realizations you had during the trip.

Task 2:

Today, you faced a significant challenge at school or work that had a profound impact on you. Write a diary entry that describes the situation in detail, expresses your emotions and thoughts about what happened, and reflects on what you learned from the experience. Consider how this challenge has affected your perspective and how you plan to move forward.

CHAPTER 6
EMAILS

AN EMAIL IS a form of electronic communication that allows individuals and organizations to send messages quickly and efficiently over the internet. Emails can be used for a wide variety of purposes, including personal communication, professional correspondence, marketing, and information sharing. Unlike traditional letters, emails are often more concise and can include attachments such as documents, images, and links.

Emails are a fundamental tool in modern communication, providing a quick and convenient way to connect with people regardless of geographical distance. They are essential for both personal and professional interactions, enabling everything from casual conversations with friends to formal business proposals and customer service inquiries.

SETTING, READERSHIP, OBJECTIVE:

- Emails can be sent from anywhere with internet access, making them versatile for both personal and professional use.
- The audience can range from friends and family to colleagues, clients, or broader professional networks.

- The goal is to communicate a message clearly and efficiently, whether it's to share information, make a request, provide updates, or maintain relationships.

STYLE AND ATTITUDE:

- Use straightforward language to convey your message effectively.
- Adjust the tone based on the relationship with the recipient and the purpose of the email (formal for professional settings, informal for personal communication).
- Maintain professionalism, especially in business correspondence, and always be courteous and respectful.

STANDARDS:

- Craft a clear and concise subject line that summarizes the email's content.
- Organize the email with clear paragraphs and headings if necessary.
- Include any necessary attachments and refer to them within the email.
- Check for grammar, spelling, and punctuation errors before sending.

TIPS AND TEMPLATES:

Writing an effective email requires clarity, brevity, and consideration of your audience. Tailor your message to the recipient, ensuring that your purpose is clear and your tone is appropriate.

- **Useful Vocabulary:** Use precise and clear language. For instance, instead of saying "I am writing to you," you could use "I wanted to reach out to you regarding…".

EMAILS

- **Idiomatic Expressions:** While idiomatic expressions can add a personal touch, they should be used sparingly and appropriately, particularly in formal emails. For example, instead of saying "Let's touch base," you could say "Let's discuss this further."

To: Recipient's email address
From: Your email address
Subject: Email subject

Greetings:
Formal Greeting: Use "Dear [Recipient's Name]" for formal emails.
Informal Greeting: Use "Hi [Recipient's Name]" or "Hello [Recipient's Name]" for informal emails.

Opening Paragraph:
State the Purpose: Clearly explain why you are writing the email.
Provide Context: Offer any necessary background information or context for your message.

Main Point 1:
Explanation: Provide details about the first main point.
Support: Include any necessary information, examples, or attachments.

Main Point 2:
Explanation: Provide details about the second main point.
Support: Include any necessary information, examples, or attachments.

Main Point 3:
Explanation: Provide details about the third main point.
Support: Include any necessary information, examples, or attachments.

Closing Paragraph:
Summarize Key Points: Briefly recap the main points discussed in the email.
Call to Action: Clearly state any desired actions or next steps.
Express Gratitude: Thank the recipient for their time or assistance.

Closing Greeting
Formal Closing: Use "Sincerely," "Best regards," or "Kind regards" for formal emails.
Informal Closing: Use "Best," "Cheers," or "Thanks" for informal emails.

Signature
Your Name Your Position or Title (if applicable)
Your Contact Information (email address, phone number)

Email Template

EMAILS

EMAIL EXAMPLE

To: Steve.Thompson@email.net
From: emily.johnson@abcdefgcorp.com
Subject: Request for Support on Upcoming Project

Dear Mr. Thompson,

I hope this email finds you well. I am writing to request your support on a new project our team is about to undertake.

As you know, we are launching a new marketing campaign for our latest product line, and I have been assigned the role of project coordinator. Given your extensive experience in digital marketing and your previous success with similar campaigns, your insights and guidance would be incredibly valuable to our team.

Specifically, I would like to ask for your assistance in the following areas:

1 Strategy Development: Helping to shape the overall strategy and identify key performance indicators (KPIs) for the campaign.

2 Content Creation: Providing input on the type of content that would resonate most with our target audience.

3 Performance Analysis: Setting up a framework for tracking the campaign's progress and making data-driven adjustments.

We are scheduled to start the project next Monday, February 29th, and I would be grateful if we could have a meeting to discuss your involvement at your earliest convenience. Your participation would not only enhance the quality of our campaign but also ensure we are aligned with the company's broader marketing objectives.

Please let me know your availability for a meeting next week. I am flexible with timing and can adjust my schedule to accommodate yours.

Thank you for considering my request. I look forward to the possibility of working together and benefiting from your expertise.

Best regards,

Emily Johnson

Marketing Coordinator

ABCDEFG Corporation

emily.johnson@abccorp.com

(123) 456-7890

EMAILS

PRACTICE TASKS

Task 1:

You recently attended a workshop on digital marketing that was very informative and beneficial for your work. Write an email to your manager, summarizing the key points you learned from the workshop and suggesting how these insights could be implemented in your company's marketing strategy. Include specific examples and propose a meeting to discuss your ideas further.

Task 2:

You are organizing a community event to raise awareness about environmental conservation. Write an email to a local business, requesting sponsorship for the event. Explain the purpose of the event, how their support would be beneficial, and the different sponsorship options available. Be sure to include a call to action, inviting them to discuss the sponsorship opportunities in more detail.

CHAPTER 7
ESSAYS

AN ESSAY IS a formal piece of writing that presents an argument, analysis, or discussion on a specific topic. Essays are integral to academic writing and are used to evaluate a student's understanding, critical thinking, and writing skills. They provide a structured way for students to express their ideas, demonstrate their knowledge, and engage with different perspectives on a given subject. Beyond academia, essays are also prevalent in professional and journalistic contexts, where they serve to present reasoned arguments, offer in-depth analyses, and explore complex issues.

ACADEMIC ESSAYS

In academic settings, essays are a fundamental component of coursework and assessments. They allow students to delve deeply into a subject, analyze various aspects of the topic, and present their findings in a coherent and structured manner. Academic essays often follow a specific format, including an introduction, body paragraphs, and a conclusion, each serving a distinct purpose. The introduction sets the stage, presenting the topic and the thesis statement, which is the main argument or focus of the essay. The body paragraphs provide detailed support for the thesis, using evidence, examples, and analysis to build a compelling argument. The conclusion summarizes the key points and reinforces the thesis, leaving the reader with a clear understanding of the essay's purpose and significance.

PROFESSIONAL ESSAYS

In professional contexts, essays are used to articulate ideas, propose solutions, and present analyses on various issues. These essays are often found in business reports, policy papers, and research studies, where they help to communicate complex information clearly and persuasively. Professional essays require a formal tone and a logical structure, ensuring that the argument is well-supported and the conclusions are based on sound evidence.

JOURNALISTIC ESSAYS

Journalistic essays, also known as opinion pieces or editorials, are common in newspapers, magazines, and online media. These essays present the writer's viewpoint on a current event, issue, or trend, aiming to persuade the reader or provoke thought. While they may include personal opinions, journalistic essays still rely on factual information and logical reasoning to support their arguments. They are typically more engaging and accessible than academic essays, using a conversational tone and rhetorical devices to connect with a broad audience.

TYPES OF ESSAYS:

Essays can be categorized into different types based on their purpose and structure:

Narrative Essays

Narrative essays tell a story or recount an event or experience in a structured manner. They focus on personal reflections and insights, using descriptive language to create a vivid picture for the reader.

Descriptive Essays

Descriptive essays provide detailed descriptions of a person, place, object, or event. They use sensory details to create an immersive experience for the reader, helping them to visualize and understand the subject.

Expository Essays

Expository essays aim to explain or inform the reader about a particular topic. They present facts, statistics, and examples without personal opinions, providing a clear and objective overview of the subject.

Persuasive Essays

Persuasive essays aim to convince the reader to adopt a particular viewpoint or take a specific action. They present logical arguments, evidence, and persuasive language to support their stance.

Analytical Essays

Analytical essays analyze a piece of literature, art, event, or phenomenon, examining its components and evaluating their significance and impact. They require critical thinking and a deep understanding of the subject.

SETTING, READERSHIP, OBJECTIVE:

- Essays are formal pieces of writing that present an argument, analyze a topic, or provide an in-depth discussion of a subject.
- The readership of an essay can vary depending on the intended audience, which could include academic peers, instructors, or a general audience interested in the topic.
- The objective of an essay is typically to persuade, inform, or educate the reader about a particular topic or issue, supported by evidence, analysis, and critical thinking.

ESSAYS

STYLE AND ATTITUDE:

- Adopts a formal and scholarly style appropriate for academic writing, with clear and concise language.
- The tone is objective, analytical, and authoritative, presenting arguments and evidence in a logical and organized manner.
- Allows for critical thinking, analysis, and interpretation of the topic or issue being discussed.

STANDARDS:

- Follows a structured format with an introduction, body paragraphs, and a conclusion, each serving a specific purpose in presenting the argument or analysis.
- Presents a clear thesis statement in the introduction that outlines the main argument or purpose of the essay.
- Supports arguments with evidence, examples, and citations from reputable sources, demonstrating research and critical thinking skills.
- Concludes with a summary of key points and a restatement of the thesis, providing closure to the essay.

TIPS AND TEMPLATES:

Writing an effective essay requires careful planning, research, and organization. Start by clearly defining your thesis statement and outlining the main points you want to address. Support your arguments with evidence and analysis, and use proper citation methods to acknowledge your sources. Revise and edit your essay for clarity, coherence, and correctness before submitting it.

- **Useful Vocabulary:** Choose words that are precise, formal, and appropriate for academic writing. Use terminology relevant to the topic and field of study, demonstrating your understanding

and expertise. Avoid vague or colloquial language, and aim for clarity and precision in your writing.
- **Idiomatic Expressions:** While idiomatic expressions may be less common in formal academic writing, you can still use language that enhances clarity and coherence. Focus on expressing your ideas clearly and logically, using transitions and connecting phrases to guide the reader through your argument or analysis.

ESSAYS

Title of Essay
Author's Name
Instructor's Name (if applicable)
Course Name (if applicable)
Date:
Abstract: (optional)

Introduction
Summary: Summarize the key points or emotions of the entry.
Future Outlook: Consider any plans, hopes, or goals for the future.
Background Information: Provide some context or background information on the topic to set the stage for your discussion.
Thesis Statement: Clearly state the main argument or purpose of the essay, giving the reader a roadmap of what to expect.

Body Paragraphs:
Topic Sentence: Each paragraph should start with a topic sentence that introduces the main idea of the paragraph.
Supporting Evidence/Examples: Provide evidence, examples, or explanations to support the topic sentence. This could include data, quotes, or detailed descriptions.
Analysis/Interpretation: Analyze the evidence and explain its relevance to the main argument. Discuss how it supports your thesis and adds to the overall understanding of the topic.

Conclusion:
Summary of Key Points: Summarize the key points discussed in the body paragraphs, reinforcing the main argument without introducing new information.
Restatement of Thesis: Restate the thesis in light of the evidence and analysis presented, showing how the argument has been
Final Thoughts or Implications: Provide a closing statement or call to action that leaves a lasting impression on the reader, possibly suggesting further research or implications of your findings.

References/Bibliography (if applicable)
Include a list of sources cited in the essay, following a consistent citation style (e.g. APA, MLA, Chicago).

Appendices (if applicable)
Appendices may include additional material such as raw data, charts, or supplementary information that supports the essay but is not essential to the main text.

Essay Template

PERSUASIVE ESSAY EXAMPLE

The Impact of Social Media on Mental Health
By Matt Fletcher

Introduction

In today's interconnected world, social media platforms like Facebook, Instagram, Twitter, and TikTok have become integral to our daily lives. They offer unprecedented opportunities for communication, entertainment, and information sharing. However, the increasing dependence on these platforms raises significant concerns about their impact on mental health. While social media provides numerous benefits, such as staying connected and fostering communities, its negative effects on mental well-being are undeniable. This essay argues that social media has a detrimental impact on mental health, primarily through social comparison, cyberbullying, and the distortion of reality.

Social Comparison

One of the most harmful effects of social media is the tendency for users to engage in social comparison. Social media platforms are flooded with images and posts showcasing idealized versions of people's lives. Users often compare their own lives to these seemingly perfect portrayals, leading to feelings of inadequacy and low self-esteem. For instance, seeing friends constantly posting about their achievements, vacations, or social outings can make individuals feel that they are not living up to the same standards. This relentless comparison fosters a sense of dissatisfaction and can contribute to depression and anxiety. It's crucial to recognize that social media often presents a curated, highlight-reel version of reality, which can be misleading and damaging to one's self-worth.

Cyberbullying and Online Harassment

Another significant issue with social media is the prevalence of cyberbullying and online harassment. Unlike traditional bullying, cyberbullying can occur 24/7 and reach a vast audience, making it relentless and inescapable for victims. The anonymity provided by social media emboldens bullies to act without fear of immediate consequences, leading to severe emotional distress for the victims. This can result in anxiety, depression, and in extreme cases, suicidal thoughts. The rise of social media has unfortunately made it easier for individuals to inflict harm on others from behind a screen, amplifying the negative impact on mental health.

Distortion of Reality

Social media also distorts reality by promoting unrealistic beauty standards and lifestyles. Filters and photo-editing tools allow users to present an altered version of themselves, creating an unattainable standard of beauty and success. This distortion of reality can lead to body image issues, eating disorders, and a constant sense of inadequacy. The pressure to look perfect and live an extraordinary life as depicted on social media can be overwhelming, particularly for impressionable young people who are still developing their sense of self. It's essential to remember that these platforms often promote a false sense of reality that can be harmful to mental health.

Conclusion

In conclusion, while social media has the potential to connect people and foster communities, its negative impact on mental health cannot be ignored. The tendency for social comparison, the rise of cyberbullying, and the distortion of reality are all significant contributors to mental health issues. It is crucial for individuals to be mindful of their social media usage and for society to promote a more balanced and realistic portrayal of life online. By fostering awareness and encouraging healthy social media habits, we can mitigate its harmful effects and enhance our overall mental well-being.

ESSAYS

PRACTICE TASKS

Task 1

Topic: The Impact of Social Media on Society

Write an expository essay discussing the impact of social media on society. Your essay should include an introduction that provides background information on the rise of social media, a clear thesis statement that outlines your main points, body paragraphs that explore the positive and negative effects of social media, and a conclusion that summarizes your key points and restates your thesis.

Task 2:

Topic: The Benefits and Drawbacks of Remote Work

Write a persuasive essay on the benefits and drawbacks of remote work. Your essay should include an introduction with a hook to engage the reader, background information on the rise of remote work, and a thesis statement that outlines your stance. The body paragraphs should present arguments and evidence supporting both the benefits and the drawbacks of remote work, followed by a conclusion that summarizes your arguments and restates your thesis, possibly offering a recommendation or prediction for the future of work.

CHAPTER 8
INTERVIEWS

AN INTERVIEW IS a structured conversation where one person (the interviewer) asks questions, and the other person (the interviewee) provides answers. Interviews are a powerful tool for gathering detailed information, personal insights, and expert opinions on a wide range of topics. They are commonly used in journalism, research, and professional contexts to explore subjects in depth, provide diverse perspectives, and uncover unique stories.

TYPES OF INTERVIEWS:

Embedded Interviews

Embedded interviews are integrated into a narrative, reading more like an article. In this format, the interviewer's questions and the interviewee's responses are woven into a story that provides context and background information. This style is often used in feature articles, profiles, and investigative journalism, where the goal is to tell a compelling story while highlighting key insights from the interviewee.

Transcribed Interviews

Transcribed interviews present a direct transcription of the conversation between the interviewer and the interviewee. This format shows everything that was mentioned during the interview, capturing the exact words, tone, and flow of the dialogue. Transcribed interviews are commonly used in academic research, professional reports, and media publications where transparency and accuracy are crucial.

SETTING, READERSHIP, OBJECTIVE:

- Interviews are conversational interactions between an interviewer and interviewee, conducted to gather insights, opinions, or expertise on a specific topic.
- The readership of an interview can vary depending on the platform or publication where it is featured, catering to audiences interested in the topic being discussed.
- The objective of an interview is to provide valuable information, perspectives, or expert opinions on a particular subject, offering readers insights and understanding.

STYLE AND ATTITUDE:

- Interviews adopt a conversational tone, facilitating a natural flow of dialogue between the interviewer and interviewee.
- The tone can vary based on the context of the interview, ranging from informal and friendly to professional and authoritative.
- Allows for spontaneity and authenticity in responses, capturing the interviewee's personality and expertise.

STANDARDS:

- Follows a structured format with questions posed by the interviewer and responses provided by the interviewee, ensuring clarity and coherence in the conversation.
- Questions are carefully crafted to elicit insightful and informative responses from the interviewee, covering various aspects of the topic.

- Encourages active listening and follow-up questions to delve deeper into key points or clarify any ambiguities.

TIPS AND TEMPLATES:

Conducting an effective interview requires preparation and research. Develop a set of well-crafted questions that align with the interview's objectives and the interviewee's expertise. Actively listen to the responses and adapt follow-up questions accordingly to explore interesting avenues or address any gaps in understanding.

- **Engaging Dialogue:** Keep the conversation lively and engaging by asking open-ended questions that encourage the interviewee to elaborate on their responses. Allow for pauses and moments of reflection, fostering a comfortable atmosphere conducive to candid discussion.
- **Respectful Interaction:** Approach the interview with professionalism and respect, recognizing the interviewee's expertise and perspective. Listen attentively, avoid interrupting, and maintain a courteous demeanour throughout the conversation.
- **Useful Vocabulary:** Use clear and direct language when asking questions. For example, "Can you explain..." or "What do you think about...?"
- **Idiomatic Expressions:** Depending on the formality of the interview, idiomatic expressions can make the conversation more relatable. For instance, "Could you shed some light on..." or "What's your take on…?"

INTERVIEWS

Interviewer's Name
Publication/Platform Name
Date of Interview:
Title of Interview:

Introduction
Context: Provide background information about the interviewee, the purpose of the interview, and the context in which it takes place. This sets the stage and helps the reader understand why the interview is significant.
Overview: Briefly outline the main topics or themes that will be covered in the interview.

Interview:
Question 1: [Question posed by the interviewer]
 Response: [Response from the interviewee]
Question 2: [Question posed by the interviewer]
 Response: [Response from the interviewee]
Question 3: [Question posed by the interviewer]
 Response: [Response from the interviewee]
[**Continue this format for all questions and responses**]

Conclusion:
Summary: Summarize key points discussed during the interview.
Final Thoughts: Include any final remarks from the interviewer or interviewee, highlighting the significance of the insights shared.

Transcribed Interview Template

Title of Interview
Interviewer's Name
Publication/Platform Name   **Date of Interview:**

Introduction:
Context: Provide background information about the interviewee, the purpose of the interview, and the context in which it takes place. This sets the stage and helps the reader understand why the interview is significant.
Overview: Briefly outline the main topics or themes that will be covered in the interview.

Section 1: Main Theme or Topic
Begin with a narrative or explanation related to the main theme or topic of this section.
Quotation 1: [Insert a relevant quote from the interviewee]
Discuss the significance of this quote, providing context and analysis.
Quotation 2: [Insert another relevant quote from the interviewee]
Continue the narrative, weaving in the interviewee's insights with contextual information and analysis.

Section 2: Another Theme or Topic
Transition to a new theme or topic, maintaining a coherent flow.
Quotation 3: [Insert a relevant quote from the interviewee]
Discuss the significance of this quote, providing context and analysis.
Quotation 4: [Insert another relevant quote from the interviewee]
Continue the narrative, weaving in the interviewee's insights with contextual information and analysis.

Continue this format for all sections/themes/topics

Conclusion
Summary: Summarize the main themes and insights shared during the interview.
Final Thoughts: Include any concluding remarks, either from the interviewer or the interviewee, that encapsulate the key takeaways from the interview.

Embedded Interview Template

INTERVIEWS

EMBEDDED INTERVIEW EXAMPLE

Overcoming Adversity: An Interview with Marathon Champion Jane Doe
By Michael Smith | May 22, 2024 | Sports Weekly

Jane Doe, a name synonymous with perseverance and triumph, recently clinched her third consecutive victory at the Anytown Marathon. In a candid interview, she shared insights into her journey, the challenges she faced, and her relentless determination to succeed.

Doe's journey to becoming a marathon champion was anything but smooth. "I remember the first time I tried to run a marathon," she recalls with a smile. "I couldn't even finish. My legs gave out, and I thought, 'This is impossible.'" But giving up was never an option for Doe. With unwavering determination, she committed to rigorous training and adopted a disciplined lifestyle.

Her training regimen is intense and highly structured. "Every morning, I start my day at 5 AM with a 10-mile run," she explains. "Consistency is key. You have to push yourself every single day." Doe also emphasizes the importance of mental strength. "There are days when your body wants to quit, but your mind has to be stronger. I always tell myself that pain is temporary, but quitting lasts forever."

Balancing her personal life with her demanding training schedule poses its own set of challenges. "It's tough," she admits. "I miss out on a lot of social events and family gatherings. But my family understands and supports my goals." Her support system plays a crucial role in her success. "I wouldn't be here without them. They keep me grounded and motivated."

Doe's story is not just about winning races but about overcoming life's obstacles with grace and tenacity. As she prepares for her next challenge, the Boston Marathon, she remains focused and optimistic. "Every race is a new beginning," she says. "You learn from every experience and come back stronger."

TRANSCRIBED INTERVIEW EXAMPLE

Overcoming Adversity: An Interview with Marathon Champion Jane Doe

By Michael Smith | May 22, 2024 | Sports Weekly

Michael Smith: Jane, congratulations on your third consecutive victory at the Anytown Marathon! How does it feel to achieve this milestone?

Jane Doe: Thank you, Michael. It feels incredible. Each victory is a testament to the hard work and dedication I've put into my training.

Michael Smith: Let's go back to the beginning. Can you tell us about your first marathon experience?

Jane Doe: Sure. I remember the first time I tried to run a marathon. I couldn't even finish. My legs gave out, and I thought, "This is impossible." But giving up was never an option for me. I knew I had to train harder and smarter.

Michael Smith: What does your training regimen look like?

Jane Doe: My training is pretty intense and highly structured. Every morning, I start my day at 5 AM with a 10-mile run. Consistency is key. You have to push yourself every single day.

Michael Smith: How do you maintain your mental strength during such rigorous training?

Jane Doe: There are days when your body wants to quit, but your mind has to be stronger. I always tell myself that pain is temporary, but quitting lasts forever. Keeping a positive mindset is crucial.

Michael Smith: Balancing personal life and such a demanding schedule must be challenging. How do you manage it?

Jane Doe: It's tough. I miss out on a lot of social events and family gatherings. But my family understands and supports my goals, which

INTERVIEWS

makes a huge difference. I wouldn't be here without them. They keep me grounded and motivated.

Michael Smith: What's next for you? Any upcoming races?

Jane Doe: I'm preparing for the Boston Marathon next. Every race is a new beginning. You learn from every experience and come back stronger. I'm excited to see what the future holds.

Michael Smith: Thank you for sharing your story with us, Jane. Best of luck with your training and future races.

Jane Doe: Thank you, Michael. It's been a pleasure.

PRACTICE TASKS

EMBEDDED INTERVIEW TASK

Task 1:

Topic: Exploring the Impact of Technology on Education

Instructions:

You have been asked to write an embedded interview for an education magazine. Your task is to interview a technology expert who has been working on integrating digital tools in classrooms. Write an article that explores the impact of technology on education by embedding quotes from the interview within your narrative.

Task 2:

Topic: The Role of Artificial Intelligence in Healthcare

Instructions:

You have been asked to write a transcribed interview for a health and technology journal. Your task is to interview a healthcare professional who specializes in using artificial intelligence (AI) to improve patient care. Transcribe the interview, capturing the exact dialogue between you and the interviewee.

CHAPTER 9
LETTERS

A LETTER IS A WRITTEN form of communication traditionally sent through the postal service, but it can also be delivered electronically. Letters are versatile and can be used for various purposes, including personal correspondence, formal business communications, invitations, and requests. They are an effective way to convey information, express feelings, make inquiries, or maintain personal and professional relationships.

Letters can be classified into different types based on their purpose and audience:

Personal Letters

These are informal letters written to friends, family members, or acquaintances. They often include personal news, updates, and casual conversation.

Formal Letters

These are structured and professional letters used for official purposes. Examples include job applications, business proposals, complaint letters, and formal requests.

Business Letters

A subset of formal letters, business letters are specifically used in professional settings to communicate with clients, employees, partners, or stakeholders.

Invitation Letters

These are letters inviting someone to an event, such as a wedding, party, or meeting. They can be either formal or informal, depending on the occasion and relationship with the recipient.

SETTING, READERSHIP, OBJECTIVE:

- **Setting:** Letters can be written and sent from anywhere, making them suitable for various contexts, including personal, academic, and professional environments.
- **Readership:** The audience can vary widely, from personal acquaintances to business associates, potential employers, and official entities.
- **Objective:** The goal is to communicate a message effectively, whether it's to inform, request, express, or invite. The tone and style of the letter should align with its purpose and the relationship with the recipient

STYLE AND ATTITUDE:

- **Formal or Informal:** Depending on the purpose and audience, letters can adopt a formal or informal style.
- **Polite and Respectful:** Maintain a courteous and respectful tone, especially in formal and business letters.
- **Clear and Concise:** Ensure the message is clear and to the point, avoiding unnecessary jargon or verbosity.

STANDARDS:

- **Proper Salutation and Closing:** Use appropriate salutations and closings based on the level of formality.

LETTERS

- **Organized Structure:** Follow a logical structure with clearly defined sections.
- **Proofreading:** Check for spelling, grammar, and punctuation errors to maintain professionalism and clarity.

NOTE

Writing a letter requires a thoughtful approach to ensure that the message is conveyed effectively and respectfully. Whether it's a heartfelt personal note or a professional business proposal, the principles of clear communication and appropriate tone are paramount.

TIPS AND TEMPLATES:

Writing an effective letter involves clarity, appropriate tone, and a structured format. Tailor your letter to the recipient and the purpose, ensuring that your message is clear and respectful.

- **Useful Vocabulary:** Use precise and appropriate language for the context. For instance, in formal letters, use phrases like "I am writing to inquire about…" or "I would like to express my gratitude…".
- **Idiomatic Expressions:** In personal letters, idiomatic expressions can add warmth and familiarity. For example, "I hope this letter finds you well" or "It's been ages since we last spoke."

IT'S ALWRITE!

Senders Address:
Name
Address
City, State, Zip Code
Email Address
Phone Number
Date

Recipient's Address:
Name
Title
Company Name
Address
City, State, Zip Code

Salutation:
Dear [Recipient's Name]

Introduction Paragraph:
Purpose: Clearly state the purpose of the letter in the opening paragraph.
Context: Provide any necessary background information or context.

Main Point 1:
Details: Explain the first main point with supporting details, examples, or evidence.

Main Point 2:
Details: Provide information about the second main point, elaborating with necessary details.

Main Point 3:
Details: Discuss the third main point, offering any additional information or insights.

Concluding Paragraph
Summary: Summarize the key points discussed in the letter.
Next Steps: Clearly state any desired actions or next steps.
Closing Remarks: Express gratitude or provide final thoughts.

Closing
Sincerely/Best regards/Kind regards,
[Your Name]

Letter Template

LETTERS

LETTER EXAMPLE

123 Maple Street

Anytown, USA 12345

May 22, 2024

Mr. John Smith

Customer Service Manager

Funland Theme Park

456 Ela Street

Anytown, USA 12345

Dear Mr. Smith,

I am writing to share my recent experience at Funland Theme Park on May 20, 2023. As a long-time patron, I was looking forward to a fun-filled day with my family, but our visit was marred by several issues.

Firstly, the wait times for rides, including Roller Coaster Express and the Ferris Wheel, were excessively long despite our Fast Passes. Additionally, popular attractions like Adventure Rapids and the Haunted Mansion were closed for maintenance without prior notice on your website, leaving us unprepared and disappointed.

Moreover, the park's cleanliness was below expected standards. Walkways and seating areas were littered with trash, and several restrooms were not adequately cleaned or stocked. Finally, at the Funland Diner, our food took over 45 minutes to arrive, and when it did, the quality was poor—cold burgers and soggy fries.

As a loyal customer, I felt it was important to bring these matters to your attention. I hope my feedback will be taken constructively and improvements will be made to enhance the visitor experience. I would appreciate a response outlining how these concerns will be addressed and some form of compensation for the inconvenience we experienced.

Thank you for taking the time to read my letter. I look forward to your response and hope our next visit to Funland Theme Park will be more enjoyable.

Sincerely,

Emily Johnson

LETTERS

PRACTICE TASKS

Task 1:

You recently stayed at a hotel where you had an excellent experience due to the exceptional service provided by the staff. Write a formal letter to the hotel manager expressing your appreciation for the service. Be sure to mention specific staff members who made your stay memorable and describe how they went above and beyond to ensure you had a pleasant experience.

Task 2:

You recently had a disappointing dining experience at a restaurant where the meal and service did not meet your expectations. Write a formal complaint letter to the restaurant manager detailing the issues you encountered. Be specific about the problems with the meal and the service, and explain how you believe the situation could be resolved or improved for future customers.

CHAPTER 10
LETTERS TO THE EDITOR

LETTERS to the editor are short, persuasive pieces written by readers in response to articles, events, or issues covered in a publication. They provide a forum for the public to express their opinions, concerns, and feedback directly to the publication's audience. These letters are an important part of democratic discourse, allowing individuals to contribute to public debate and share their perspectives on a wide range of topics.

SETTING, READERSHIP, AND OBJECTIVE:

- **Setting:** Letters to the editor are published in newspapers, magazines, and online platforms, typically in a designated section for reader responses. They are submitted by readers who wish to share their views on topics of public interest.
- **Readership:** The readership includes the publication's audience, which can range from local community members to a national or international readership, depending on the publication's reach.
- **Objective:** The primary goal of a letter to the editor is to express a specific viewpoint, advocate for a particular position, or provide feedback on articles or issues covered by the

publication. It aims to influence public opinion, contribute to ongoing discussions, and encourage action or change.

STYLE AND ATTITUDE:

- **Style:** Letters to the editor adopt a concise and direct style. The writing is clear and focused, often addressing a single issue or point. The language used is accessible and engaging, aiming to communicate the writer's message effectively.
- **Attitude:** The tone of a letter to the editor can vary based on the writer's perspective and the nature of the topic. It can be passionate and assertive, critical and analytical, or supportive and appreciative, depending on the message the writer wishes to convey.

STANDARDS:

- **Structure:** Follows a structured format with an introduction referencing the article or issue being addressed, body paragraphs elaborating on the writer's viewpoint, and a conclusion summarizing key points or suggesting a course of action.
- **Clarity and Logic:** Arguments or opinions are presented in a clear and logical manner, with evidence or reasoning to support the writer's position.
- **Brevity:** Letters to the editor are typically brief, focusing on a single point or argument. They usually range from a few sentences to a few paragraphs.
- **Relevance:** The letters address specific articles, issues, or events that have been recently covered by the publication. They often reference the original content to provide context.

TIPS AND TEMPLATES:

- Writing an effective letter to the editor involves brevity, relevance, and a clear focus on a single issue. Clearly state your viewpoint or argument, provide concise evidence or examples to support your position, and suggest actionable solutions or recommendations.
- **Brevity and Focus:** Keep the letter brief and to the point, addressing a single issue or topic. Avoid long-winded explanations or multiple arguments, as letters to the editor have limited space.
- **Relevance:** Make sure your letter directly responds to a specific article, issue, or event covered by the publication. Reference the original content to provide context and ensure your letter is timely and relevant.
- **Clarity and Precision:** Use clear and straightforward language to convey your message. Avoid jargon and complex sentences. Be precise in your arguments and provide concise evidence or examples to support your viewpoint.
- **Engaging Opening:** Start with a strong opening sentence to capture the reader's attention. Clearly state the purpose of your letter and your main argument or viewpoint.
- **Polite and Respectful Tone:** Even if you are criticizing or disagreeing with the original content, maintain a respectful and polite tone. Constructive criticism is more likely to be published and taken seriously.
- **Call to Action:** End with a clear conclusion or call to action, suggesting what should be done or what you hope will change as a result of your letter.
- **Useful Vocabulary:** Choose words that are impactful and persuasive, enhancing the effectiveness of your letter. Examples include "imperative," "commend," "address," "highlight," "emphasize," etc.
- **Idiomatic Expressions:** Incorporate idiomatic expressions to add depth and nuance to your writing, making it more engaging and memorable for the reader. Examples include "get

to the heart of the matter," "shed light on," "hit home," "raise a red flag," etc.

———

Senders Address:
Name
Address
City, State, Zip Code
Email Address
Phone Number
Date

Recipient's Address:
Editor's Name
Publication Name
Publication Address
City, State, Zip Code

Subject (Brief Subject of Letter):

Salutation:
Dear [Recipient's Name]

Introduction Paragraph:
Reference the article or issue you are responding to, including the publication date or title if relevant. State your main argument or viewpoint clearly and concisely.

First Point:
Present your first argument or perspective related to the issue.
Provide supporting evidence, examples, or personal experiences.

Second Point:
Present your second argument or perspective.
Provide additional evidence or examples to support your viewpoint.

Third Point (If applicable):
Present any additional arguments or perspectives.
Support with relevant evidence or examples.

Concluding Paragraph
Summarize your key points or arguments.
Reiterate your main message or call to action, suggesting what should be done or what you hope will change as a result of your letter.

Sincerely:
Your Name

Letter to Editor Template

LETTERS TO THE EDITOR

EXAMPLE LETTER TO THE EDITOR

John Doe

123 Main Street

Anytown, USA 12345

johndoe@example.com

May 20, 2024

Jane Smith

Editor, Anytown Times

456 Publication Road

Anytown, USA 12345

Subject: Concern Over Proposed Park Renovation Plan

Dear Ms. Smith,

I am writing in response to the recent article titled "City Proposes Major Renovation for Central Park" published on May 15, 2024. While the intention behind the renovation plan is commendable, I have serious concerns about its potential impact on the local wildlife and community access.

The proposed plan includes the removal of several mature trees that serve as a habitat for various bird species. These trees are not only vital for the local ecosystem but also enhance the natural beauty of the park. Removing them would disrupt the habitat and potentially drive away the wildlife that residents and visitors enjoy.

Furthermore, the plan's budget allocation heavily favors new recreational facilities at the expense of maintaining existing green spaces. While modern amenities are attractive, it is crucial to preserve the park's natural areas that provide a tranquil environment for relaxation and recreation. Many community members, particularly the elderly and those with young children, prefer these quiet spaces.

In conclusion, I urge the city council to reconsider the current renovation plan and seek a balanced approach that prioritizes both new developments and the preservation of our park's natural elements. Ensuring the protection of our local wildlife and green spaces will benefit the entire community for generations to come.

Sincerely,

John Doe

PRACTICE TASKS

Task 1:

You have recently read an article in your local newspaper about the proposed construction of a new shopping mall in your neighborhood. You are concerned about the potential impact this development might have on the local environment and the community. Write a letter to the editor expressing your concerns, providing evidence to support your viewpoint, and suggesting alternatives or solutions.

Task 2:

You recently read a glowing review of a new book in your favorite literary magazine. However, after reading the book yourself, you were disappointed with its content and quality. Write a letter to the editor of the magazine, expressing your critique of the book, pointing out specific issues you found, and offering an alternative perspective on the review.

CHAPTER 11
NEWS REPORTS

A NEWS REPORT is a factual and concise account of a recent event or development, intended to inform the public about significant occurrences in an objective and straightforward manner. News reports are a fundamental component of journalism and are essential for keeping the public informed about local, national, and international events. They cover a wide range of topics, including politics, business, sports, entertainment, and more, presenting information in a clear and accessible format.

Purpose of a News Report

The primary purpose of a news report is to provide accurate, timely, and relevant information to the audience. It aims to inform the public about events or developments that have occurred, presenting the facts without bias or personal opinions. News reports help readers stay informed about what is happening in their community and around the world, allowing them to make informed decisions and stay engaged with current events.

Key Characteristics:

- **Objectivity:** News reports are written in an objective tone,

presenting facts without bias or personal opinion. The goal is to inform rather than persuade or entertain.
- **Timeliness:** News reports focus on recent events or developments, emphasizing the importance of timely information. They are often published shortly after the event occurs to provide the most up-to-date information.
- **Clarity and Conciseness:** News reports are written in clear and concise language, making it easy for readers to understand the key points quickly. They avoid unnecessary details and focus on the most important information.
- **Structure:** News reports follow a specific structure, starting with a headline and lead paragraph (lede) that summarize the main points, followed by body paragraphs that provide additional details and context. The information is often presented in order of importance, with the most critical details appearing first.

SETTING, READERSHIP, OBJECTIVE:

- News reports are concise, factual accounts of recent events or developments, intended to inform the public about significant occurrences.
- The readership of a news report typically includes a broad audience interested in staying informed about current events, ranging from local communities to global audiences.
- The objective of a news report is to provide accurate, timely information about an event or issue, presenting key facts and developments in an accessible and engaging manner.

STYLE AND ATTITUDE:

- News reports adopt a formal and objective style, presenting information in a straightforward and impartial manner.
- The tone is factual and neutral, avoiding bias or opinionated commentary to ensure credibility and objectivity.

- Allows for clarity and conciseness in conveying essential information, prioritizing accuracy and relevance.

STANDARDS:

- Follows a structured format with a headline, lead paragraph (or "lede"), body paragraphs providing additional details, and a conclusion summarizing key points.
- Presents information in a clear, logical sequence, organizing details based on their importance and relevance to the story.
- Sources information from reliable and reputable sources, verifying facts to ensure accuracy and credibility.

TIPS AND TEMPLATES:

Writing an effective news report requires thorough research and adherence to journalistic principles. Gather information from multiple sources, including eyewitnesses, officials, and experts, to provide a comprehensive account of the event. Ensure accuracy by fact-checking and corroborating details before publication.

- **Clarity and Brevity:** Keep the report concise and focused, prioritizing essential information and avoiding unnecessary details. Use clear, straightforward language to convey facts and developments accurately.
- **Objectivity and Balance:** Maintain impartiality and avoid inserting personal opinions or biases into the report. Present multiple perspectives if applicable, allowing readers to form their own conclusions based on the facts presented.
- **Useful Vocabulary:** Incorporate precise and descriptive language to enhance the clarity and impact of your news report. Examples include "alleged," "confirmed," "unprecedented," "surge," "unveiled," etc.
- **Idiomatic Expressions:** While idiomatic expressions may be less common in news reports, they can add nuance and emphasis to your writing. Examples include "on the brink of,"

NEWS REPORTS

"in the aftermath," "a storm of controversy," "at the forefront," etc.

IT'S ALWRITE!

HEADLINE

Date of Publication | Publication Name | Reports Name

Lead Paragraph:
Brief summary of the main event or development.

Answers the key questions of who, what, when, where, why, and how.

Body Paragraph:
Provide additional details and context, organized logically.

Include quotes from relevant sources, eyewitnesses, or experts.

Use clear and concise language to present the facts.

Conclusion:
Summarize key points and implications of the event.

Provide any additional information or updates.

Images Optional

News Report Template

NEWS REPORTS

NEWS REPORT EXAMPLE

Major Fire Breaks Out in Downtown Commercial Building

By Sarah Johnson | May 21, 2024 | Anytown Times

Anytown, USA – A significant fire erupted in a downtown commercial building late last night, causing extensive damage and prompting the evacuation of nearby buildings. The fire, which started around 11:30 PM, engulfed the four-story structure known for housing several local businesses, including a popular restaurant and a small tech startup.

Firefighters responded quickly to the scene, but the intensity of the blaze made containment difficult. By early morning, the fire was largely under control, but not before it had caused significant damage to the building and its contents.

Details of the Incident

According to Fire Chief Mark Thompson, the fire is believed to have started on the second floor, where the restaurant is located. "Our initial investigation suggests that the fire may have been caused by an electrical fault in the kitchen area," said Thompson. "We are continuing to investigate the exact cause, but at this point, there is no indication of foul play."

Impact on Businesses

The building is home to six businesses, all of which have suffered varying degrees of damage. The restaurant, which had just celebrated its fifth anniversary, is among the hardest hit. "It's devastating," said owner Maria Lopez. "We put our heart and soul into this place, and seeing it like this is heartbreaking. But we are grateful that no one was hurt."

· · ·

Evacuation and Safety Measures

The fire prompted the evacuation of several nearby buildings, including residential apartments and other commercial properties. Firefighters and emergency personnel worked throughout the night to ensure the safety of all residents. No injuries have been reported so far, but some residents were treated on-site for smoke inhalation.

Community Response

As news of the fire spread, community members began to rally support for the affected businesses. A crowdfunding campaign has already been set up to help those impacted by the fire. "This community is incredibly resilient," said local council member John Davis. "We will come together to support our neighbors and help rebuild what was lost."

The fire department has urged the public to stay clear of the area while cleanup and investigations are ongoing. More updates will be provided as new information becomes available. Residents with any information related to the fire are encouraged to contact the Anytown Fire Department.

NEWS REPORTS

PRACTICE TASKS

Task 1:

Topic: Annual Charity Run Raises Funds for Local Hospital

Instructions:

Write a news report about the annual charity run that took place in your local community last weekend. The event aimed to raise funds for the local hospital and saw participation from various community members, including local celebrities, school children, and senior citizens. Your report should include details about the event, the amount of money raised, quotes from participants and organizers, and the impact of the funds on the hospital.

Task 2:

Topic: Major Storm Causes Power Outages and Damage Across the City

Instructions:

Write a news report on a major storm that hit your city last night, causing widespread power outages and significant damage to homes and infrastructure. Your report should include details about the extent of the damage, responses from local authorities and emergency services, quotes from affected residents, and information on recovery efforts.

CHAPTER 12
OFFICIAL REPORTS

OFFICIAL REPORTS ARE comprehensive documents designed to present detailed information, findings, and recommendations on specific topics or issues. These reports are used across various sectors, including government, business, academia, and non-profit organizations. Their primary purpose is to inform decision-makers, stakeholders, and the general public about significant developments, performance metrics, research outcomes, or policy evaluations. Official reports are characterized by their formal tone, structured layout, and reliance on data and evidence to support their conclusions. They play a crucial role in transparency, accountability, and informed decision-making, ensuring that actions and policies are based on accurate and thorough analysis.

SETTING, READERSHIP, OBJECTIVE:

- Formal reports are comprehensive documents used to present findings, analyses, or recommendations on a specific topic or issue.
- The readership of a formal report typically includes stakeholders, decision-makers, or experts with an interest in the topic being addressed.

- The objective of a formal report is to provide accurate, detailed information and analysis to support decision-making, policy development, or problem-solving.

STYLE AND ATTITUDE:

- Formal reports adopt a professional and objective tone, conveying authority, credibility, and expertise in the subject matter.
- The style is structured and organized, with clear headings, sections, and subheadings to facilitate understanding and navigation.
- Allows for thorough research, analysis, and documentation of findings, ensuring accuracy, reliability, and relevance.

STANDARDS:

- Follows a structured format with an introduction providing background information and objectives, body sections presenting findings, analysis, and recommendations, and a conclusion summarizing key points and implications.
- Presents information in a clear, logical manner, using data, evidence, and visuals to support analysis and conclusions.
- Adheres to professional standards and guidelines for report writing, including citation of sources, adherence to formatting conventions, and consideration of ethical considerations.

TIPS AND TEMPLATES:

Writing an effective formal report requires careful planning, research, and attention to detail. Tailor your report to the needs and preferences of the audience, providing relevant information and analysis to support decision-making or problem-solving.

- **Clarity and Precision:** Clearly articulate the purpose, scope, and findings of the report, using precise language and terminology to convey meaning accurately. Avoid ambiguity or vague statements, ensuring that each point is clearly defined and supported.
- **Professionalism:** Maintain a professional tone and demeanor throughout your report, demonstrating objectivity, impartiality, and respect for diverse perspectives. Use formal language and structure to convey professionalism and expertise.
- **Useful Vocabulary:** Incorporate words and phrases that convey professionalism, accuracy, and authority in the subject matter. Examples include "analysis," "findings," "recommendations," "implications," "conclusions," etc.
- **Idiomatic Expressions:** While idiomatic expressions may be less common in formal reports, you can still use language that enhances clarity and engagement. Examples include "in the long run," "in light of," "take into account," "as a result of," etc.

OFFICIAL REPORTS

Report Title
Date:

Your Name
Your Position or Title
Your Organization
Your Contact Information

[Recipient's Name]
[Recipient's Position or Title]
[Recipient's Organization]
[Recipient's Contact Information]

Table of Contents:
List of sections and subsections with page numbers

List of Figures/Tables/Appendices (if applicable):
List of figures, tables, or appendices with corresponding page numbers

Executive Summary:
Brief overview of the report's purpose, scope, findings, and recommendations

Introduction:
- Provide background information and context for the report
- Outline the objectives and scope of the report

Body Sections:

1. Literature Review:
Review of relevant literature, theories, or frameworks

2. Methodology:
Description of research methods, data collection, and analysis procedures

3. Findings:
Presentation of research findings, data analysis, or case studies

4. Analysis:
Interpretation and analysis of findings, identifying patterns, trends, or relationships

5. Recommendations:
Proposed actions or strategies based on the analysis and findings

Conclusion
- Summarize key findings, conclusions and recommendations
- Highlight implications for decision-making or future research

References/Bibliography
Appendices

Official Report Template

EXAMPLE REPORT

Official Report on the Implementation of the School Recycling Program

Greenwood High School
Date: May 30, 2021
Prepared by: Emily Johnson
Position: Student Council President

Executive Summary:

This report evaluates the implementation and impact of the newly established recycling program at Greenwood High School. The initiative aimed to reduce waste, promote environmental awareness, and engage students in sustainable practices. The report details the program's objectives, execution, outcomes, and recommendations for future improvements.

Introduction:

In response to growing concerns about environmental sustainability, Greenwood High School launched a recycling program in January 2024. The program was designed to reduce waste, increase recycling rates, and educate students about the importance of environmental conservation.

This report aims to assess the effectiveness of the recycling program, identify successes and challenges, and provide recommendations for enhancing the program's impact.

Objectives of the Recycling Program:

1. Reduce the amount of waste sent to landfills.

2. Increase the recycling rate of paper, plastic, and metal materials.

3. Educate students and staff about sustainable practices and the importance of recycling.

Methodology:

Data Collection

Data was collected through waste audits, surveys, and feedback from students and staff. The program's performance was measured by comparing waste and recycling volumes before and after implementation.

Analysis

The collected data was analyzed to determine the program's effectiveness in meeting its objectives.

Findings:

- **Reduction in Waste:** The volume of waste sent to landfills decreased by 30% within the first three months of the program.
- **Increased Recycling Rates:** The recycling rate increased by 45%, with significant improvements in paper and plastic recycling.
- **Student and Staff Engagement:** Surveys indicated that 80% of students and staff participated in the recycling program and reported increased awareness of sustainable practices.

Challenges:

- **Contamination:** Some recycling bins contained non-recyclable materials, indicating a need for better education on proper recycling practices.
- **Resource Allocation:** Limited resources for managing and maintaining the program, including a need for more recycling bins and educational materials.

Recommendations:

- **Enhanced Education:** Implement regular workshops and information sessions to educate students and staff on proper recycling practices.
- **Increase Resources:** Allocate additional resources for recycling bins, signage, and promotional materials to support the program.
- **Ongoing Monitoring:** Establish a monitoring system to track the program's progress and make necessary adjustments.

Conclusion

The implementation of the recycling program at Greenwood High School has been largely successful, with significant reductions in waste and increases in recycling rates. However, there are areas for improvement, particularly in education and resource allocation. By addressing these challenges, the program can continue to grow and have a more substantial impact on the school's sustainability efforts.

Emily Johnson | Student Council President

Contact Information:

emily.johnson@greenwoodhigh.edu

OFFICIAL REPORTS

PRACTICE TASKS:

Task 1: Evaluation of a New School Policy

Your school recently implemented a new policy requiring students to wear uniforms. Write an official report evaluating the implementation and impact of this policy. Your report should include the objectives of the policy, the methodology used to gather data, findings on the policy's effectiveness, challenges encountered, and recommendations for improvement. Ensure your report is well-structured and provides clear evidence to support your conclusions.

Task 2: Assessment of a School Event

Your school hosted a large community event aimed at promoting health and wellness among students and their families. Write an official report assessing the success of this event. Include the objectives of the event, the methods used to evaluate its success (such as surveys, attendance records, and feedback forms), the key findings, any challenges or issues that arose, and recommendations for future events. Make sure to present your information in a clear, concise, and organized manner.

CHAPTER 13
OPINION COLUMNS

OPINION COLUMNS ARE a form of persuasive writing that allows writers to express their viewpoints, insights, and arguments on various topics. These columns are a staple in newspapers, magazines, and online publications, offering a platform for writers to share their personal perspectives on current events, societal issues, or other matters of public interest. Unlike news reports, which focus on presenting factual information, opinion columns are meant to provoke thought, inspire debate, and influence public opinion. They often reflect the voice and personality of the writer, making them distinct and engaging.

SETTING, READERSHIP, OBJECTIVE:

- Opinion columns are written expressions of personal viewpoints, opinions, or perspectives on various issues or events.
- The readership of an opinion column typically includes the audience of the publication where it is featured, ranging from local communities to national or international readers.
- The objective of an opinion column is to express a specific

viewpoint, advocate for a particular position, or provide commentary on current events or societal issues.

Style and Attitude:

- Opinion columns adopt a conversational yet persuasive style, engaging the reader with the author's viewpoint.
- The tone can vary based on the author's perspective and the nature of the topic, ranging from impassioned and assertive to thoughtful and reflective.
- Allows for personal anecdotes, examples, or experiences to support the author's argument or perspective.

Standards:

- Follows a structured format with an introduction presenting the topic or issue, body paragraphs elaborating on the author's viewpoint, and a conclusion summarizing key points or offering a call to action.
- Presents arguments or opinions in a clear and logical manner, providing evidence or reasoning to support the author's position.
- Acknowledges opposing viewpoints or counterarguments and offers rebuttals or refutations when appropriate.

TIPS AND TEMPLATES:

Writing an effective opinion column requires clarity, coherence, and persuasive argumentation. Clearly state your viewpoint or argument, provide evidence or examples to support your position, and offer solutions or recommendations when addressing issues.

- **Clarity and Conciseness:** Keep the column concise and focused, addressing a single issue or topic in depth. Use clear and straightforward language to convey your message effectively.

- **Persuasive Techniques:** Use rhetorical devices such as ethos, pathos, and logos to appeal to the reader's emotions, credibility, and logic, respectively. Incorporate persuasive language and compelling arguments to sway the reader's opinion or inspire action.
- **Useful Vocabulary:** Choose words that are impactful and persuasive, enhancing the effectiveness of your column. Examples include "injustice," "inequality," "advocate," "empower," "transform," etc.
- **Idiomatic Expressions:** Incorporate idiomatic expressions to add depth and nuance to your writing, making it more engaging and memorable for the reader. Examples include "food for thought," "a blessing in disguise," "turn a blind eye," "at the end of the day," etc.

COLUMN TITLE

Authors Name | Date:

Introduction

Hook: Start with a strong opening sentence or a compelling question to grab the reader's attention.

Context: Provide background information or context for the topic being discussed.

Thesis Statement: Clearly state your main argument or viewpoint.

Main Point 1:
Present the first main argument or perspective.
Provide supporting evidence, examples, or anecdotes.
Analyze and explain the significance of this point.

Main Point 2:
Present the second main argument or perspective.
Provide additional evidence, examples, or anecdotes.
Analyze and explain the significance of this point.

Main Point 3 (if applicable):
Present the third main argument or perspective.
Provide additional evidence, examples, or anecdotes.
Analyze and explain the significance of this point.

Counterarguments and Rebuttals:

Counterargument 1:
Present a common counterargument or opposing viewpoint.
Provide a rebuttal or refutation of this counterargument.

Counterargument 2 (if applicable):
Present another counterargument or opposing viewpoint.
Provide a rebuttal or refutation of this counterargument.

Conclusion:

Summary: Summarize the key points made in the column.
Restate Thesis: Restate your main argument or viewpoint.
Call to Action or Final Thought: End with a call to action, a thought-provoking question, or a memorable closing statement.

Opinion Column Template

OPINION COLUMN EXAMPLE

The Case Against the New Shopping Mall
By Jane Smith | May 20, 2024

The recent proposal to construct a new shopping mall in our neighborhood has sparked a heated debate among residents. While some see it as a sign of progress and economic growth, I believe that the potential negative impacts far outweigh the benefits. This column will argue that building the shopping mall will harm our local environment and disrupt the community's character.

One of the most significant concerns is the environmental impact of the proposed mall. The construction process will involve clearing a large area of green space, which currently serves as a habitat for local wildlife. Studies have shown that such developments lead to habitat loss and decreased biodiversity. Additionally, the increased traffic and pollution resulting from the mall will further degrade our local environment.

The mall will also disrupt the tight-knit character of our community. Small, locally-owned businesses that define our neighborhood are unlikely to survive the competition from large retail chains. These businesses provide not only goods and services but also a sense of identity and community spirit. Replacing them with impersonal chain stores will erode the unique charm that makes our neighborhood special.

Proponents of the mall argue that it will bring economic benefits, such as job creation and increased tax revenue. However, these benefits are often overstated. Many of the jobs created will be low-wage positions, and the tax revenue generated may not be enough to offset the costs of increased infrastructure and public service demands.

Another common argument is that the mall will provide convenient shopping options for residents. While convenience is important, it should not come at the cost of our environment and community. There are alternative ways to enhance local shopping options without resorting to large-scale developments.

In conclusion, while the proposed shopping mall may seem like a step forward, it poses significant risks to our environment and community. I urge local officials and residents to reconsider this project and explore more sustainable and community-friendly alternatives. At the end of the day, preserving the character and health of our neighborhood should be our top priority.

PRACTICE TASKS:

Task 1:

You have noticed that your local government is planning to cut funding for public libraries in your community. You believe that public libraries are essential for education and community well-being. Write an opinion column for your local newspaper where you argue against the funding cuts, provide evidence to support your stance, and suggest alternative ways to address budget concerns without sacrificing library services.

Task 2:

The popularity of electric scooters has been rising in your city, with many people seeing them as a convenient and eco-friendly mode of transportation. However, you have concerns about their safety and the clutter they create on sidewalks. Write an opinion column for a local magazine where you discuss the pros and cons of electric scooters, present your viewpoint on their use, and propose solutions to address the issues you see.

CHAPTER 14
PROPOSALS

PROPOSALS ARE formal documents that outline plans, ideas, or projects intended to persuade the audience to support or approve a particular initiative. They play a crucial role in a wide range of settings, including business, academia, research, and nonprofit organizations. In business, proposals are often used to pitch new projects, request funding, or suggest strategic changes. In academia and research, they are essential for securing grants, initiating studies, or gaining approval for academic programs. Nonprofits use proposals to seek donations, sponsorships, or partnerships to support their causes. A well-crafted proposal not only presents a clear and compelling argument but also demonstrates the proposer's thorough understanding of the subject matter, meticulous planning, and the ability to deliver the proposed outcomes successfully.

SETTING, READERSHIP, OBECTIVE:

- Proposals are used in diverse environments such as businesses seeking project approval or funding, researchers applying for grants, students proposing a thesis, and nonprofits requesting support from donors.

- The readership of a proposal includes decision-makers, stakeholders, funding bodies, supervisors, or any individuals responsible for approving or funding the proposed project. This audience is often looking for clear, concise, and compelling reasons to support the initiative.
- The primary objective of a proposal is to convince the reader of the feasibility and value of the proposed plan. It aims to demonstrate that the proposer has a well-thought-out strategy, a thorough understanding of the problem or opportunity, and the capability to successfully execute the plan.

STYLE AND ATTITUDE:

- Proposals adopt a formal and professional style, using clear and precise language to present the plan. The writing should be structured and logical, guiding the reader through the rationale, methodology, and expected outcomes of the proposal.
- The tone should be confident and persuasive, demonstrating the proposer's expertise and enthusiasm for the project. It should convey a sense of urgency and importance, encouraging the reader to take action in support of the proposal.

STANDARDS:

- Begins with an engaging introduction that outlines the problem or opportunity and states the purpose of the proposal.
- Provides context and justification for the proposal, explaining why it is necessary and how it addresses a specific need or opportunity.
- Clearly outlines the goals and objectives of the proposal, specifying what the proposer aims to achieve.
- Details the proposed plan of action, including the methods,

strategies, and steps that will be taken to achieve the objectives.
- Includes a detailed budget and outlines the resources required to implement the proposal, justifying the costs and demonstrating cost-effectiveness.
- Provides a realistic timeline for the completion of the project, highlighting key milestones and deliverables.
- Summarizes the key points of the proposal, reiterates the benefits, and makes a final persuasive appeal for support or approval.

TIPS AND TEMPLATES:

- Clearly articulate the proposed plan, idea, or project, providing sufficient detail to convey its feasibility and potential benefits without overwhelming the reader with unnecessary information.
- Maintain a professional tone and demeanor throughout your proposal, demonstrating expertise, credibility, and confidence in the proposed solution or approach. Use formal language and structure to convey professionalism and competence.
- Incorporate words and phrases that convey professionalism, expertise, and confidence in the proposed plan or idea. Examples include "innovative," "strategic," "cost-effective," "sustainable," "competitive advantage," etc.
- While idiomatic expressions may be less common in formal documents like proposals, you can still use language that enhances clarity and engagement. Examples include "break new ground," "raise the bar," "cutting-edge," "turnkey solution," etc.

IT'S ALWRITE!

Proposal Title:
Date:
Your Name
Your Position or Title
Your Organization
Your Contact Information

Recipient's Name:
Recipient's Position or Title
Recipient's Organization:
Recipient's Contact Information:

Executive Summary:
Brief overview of the proposed plan, idea, or project
Highlight key objectives and benefits
Mention the desired action or approval from the recipient

Introduction:
Background Information: Provide background information and context for the proposal
Purpose: State the purpose of the proposal and what it aims to achieve
Problem Statement: Describe the problem or opportunity that the proposal addresses

Objectives:
Primary Objective: Clearly outline the main goal of the proposal
Secondary Objectives: List any additional goals that support the primary objective

Methodology & Plan:
Plan of Action: Detail the proposed plan, including methods, strategies, and steps
Implementation: Explain how the plan will be implemented, including resources and personnel involved
Timeline: Provide a realistic timeline for the completion of the project, highlighting key milestones and deliverables

Budget & Resources
Detailed Budget: Include a detailed budget, itemizing costs associated with the proposal
Resource Allocation: Outline the resources required to implement the proposal, justifying the costs and demonstrating cost-effectiveness

Proposal Template (1 of 2)

PROPOSALS

Evaluation and Metrics:
Evaluation Plan: Explain how the success of the proposal will be evaluated
Metrics: List the metrics that will be used to measure the outcomes and impact of the proposal

Conclusion:
Summary of Key Points: Summarize the main points discussed in the proposal
Restate Benefits: Reiterate the benefits and positive impact of the proposal
Call to Action: Make a final persuasive appeal for support or approval, specifying the desired next steps

Closing:
Thank You: Thank the recipient for considering the proposal
Contact Information: Provide your contact information for further inquiries

Appendices (If applicable)
- Include any additional supporting material, such as charts, graphs, or detailed data

Proposal Template (2 of 2)

EXAMPLE PROPOSAL

Proposal for Meat-Free Monday in the School Canteen

May 25, 2023
Emily Johnson
Student Council President
Greenwood High School
emily.johnson@greenwoodhigh.edu

Mr. David Thompson
Principal
Greenwood High School
123 Education Lane
Greenwood, State, ZIP Code

Executive Summary:

This proposal recommends the introduction of "Meat-Free Monday" in the Greenwood High School canteen. The initiative aims to promote environmental sustainability, encourage healthy eating habits, and reduce the school's carbon footprint. By offering a variety of nutritious vegetarian meals once a week, we hope to educate students about the benefits of plant-based diets and inspire positive dietary changes.

Introduction:

Greenwood High School has always been at the forefront of promoting healthy lifestyles and sustainable practices among students. As part of our ongoing efforts to enhance our school's environmental responsibility, we propose implementing a "Meat-Free Monday" initiative in the school canteen.

The purpose of this proposal is to outline the benefits of adopting a Meat-Free Monday program, provide a plan for implementation, and demonstrate how this initiative aligns with our school's commitment to health and sustainability.

The consumption of meat has significant environmental impacts, including high greenhouse gas emissions, deforestation, and water usage. Additionally, there is a growing awareness of the health benefits associated with plant-based diets. By reducing meat consumption, we can contribute to environmental preservation and promote healthier eating habits among students.

Background and Rationale:

Implementing Meat-Free Monday will reduce the school's carbon footprint, promote environmental awareness, and encourage students to explore nutritious vegetarian options. Research indicates that reducing meat consumption, even by one day a week, can significantly impact the environment and public health.

Studies show that the livestock industry is a major contributor to greenhouse gas emissions, accounting for approximately 14.5% of global emissions. Additionally, plant-based diets have been linked to lower risks of chronic diseases such as heart disease, diabetes, and certain cancers.

Objectives:

- To introduce Meat-Free Monday in the school canteen, providing healthy vegetarian meal options once a week.
- To educate students about the environmental and health benefits of reducing meat consumption and to foster a culture of sustainability within the school community

Methodology/Plan:

- Collaborate with the canteen staff to develop a diverse and appealing vegetarian menu.
- Conduct a survey to gather student feedback on preferred vegetarian dishes.

- Launch an awareness campaign to inform students and staff about the initiative and its benefits.

Implementation:

- Begin with a pilot program for one month, offering vegetarian meals every Monday.
- Gather feedback and adjust the menu based on student preferences and nutritional guidelines.

Timeline:

- June 2024: Plan and develop the vegetarian menu.
- July 2024: Conduct student surveys and launch the awareness campaign.
- August 2024: Implement the pilot program and gather feedback.
- September 2024: Evaluate the pilot program and make necessary adjustments for full implementation.

Budget and Resources:

- Ingredients for vegetarian meals: $500 per month
- Promotional materials for the awareness campaign: $200
- Training sessions for canteen staff: $300
- Collaboration with local suppliers to source fresh, affordable vegetarian ingredients.
- Allocation of existing canteen staff to prepare and serve the vegetarian meals.

Evaluation and Metrics

Evaluation Plan:

- Monitor student participation and satisfaction through surveys and feedback forms.

PROPOSALS

- Track the environmental impact by measuring reductions in meat consumption and related carbon emissions.

Metrics:

- Number of students opting for vegetarian meals on Mondays.
- Student feedback ratings on meal quality and satisfaction.
- Quantitative data on meat consumption and environmental impact.

Conclusion:

Introducing Meat-Free Monday at Greenwood High School will promote environmental sustainability, encourage healthier eating habits, and align with our school's commitment to responsible practices.

This initiative will reduce our carbon footprint, educate students about the benefits of plant-based diets, and foster a culture of sustainability.

We urge the school administration to approve this proposal and support the implementation of Meat-Free Monday, starting with a pilot program in August 2024.

Thank you for considering this proposal. We look forward to your support in making Greenwood High School a leader in health and sustainability.

For further inquiries, please contact Emily Johnson at emily.johnson@greenwoodhigh.edu or 555-678-9101.

PRACTICE TASKS:

Task 1: School Recycling Program

Your school currently does not have a structured recycling program, and you are passionate about implementing one to reduce waste and promote environmental awareness. Write a proposal to the school administration outlining the benefits of a recycling program, the steps needed to implement it, and how it will be maintained. Be sure to include details about the types of materials to be recycled, potential costs, and any partnerships with local recycling companies.

Task 2: Introducing a New After-School Club

You have noticed that there is a growing interest among students in coding and technology, but there is no after-school club that focuses on these areas. Write a proposal to the school principal suggesting the creation of a Coding and Technology Club. Include the objectives of the club, the benefits for students, a plan for meeting times and activities, potential costs, and how you plan to attract members and sustain the club over time.

CHAPTER 15
REVIEWS

A REVIEW IS a critical evaluation or analysis of a product, service, event, or creative work, such as a book, film, or performance. Reviews are designed to provide readers with an informed opinion about the subject, helping them make decisions about whether to purchase, attend, or engage with it. Reviews can be found in various formats, including articles, blogs, and videos, and they appear in a range of publications, from newspapers and magazines to online platforms and personal blogs.

The primary purpose of a review is to offer an objective assessment based on the reviewer's experience and expertise. Reviews typically cover key aspects such as quality, value, and effectiveness, and they often include both positive and negative points. The reviewer's goal is to present a balanced and fair evaluation, supported by evidence and examples, to guide the reader's judgment.

Reviews adopt a persuasive yet informative style, aiming to engage the reader while providing valuable insights. The tone can vary from casual and conversational to formal and analytical, depending on the context and audience. Effective reviews are clear, concise, and well-structured, making it easy for readers to understand the reviewer's perspective and conclusions.

SETTING, READERSHIP, OBJECTIVE:

- Reviews are evaluative analyses or critiques of various works, products, or experiences, intended to inform and guide potential consumers or audiences.
- The readership of a review typically includes consumers, audiences, or enthusiasts interested in the subject being reviewed, seeking informed opinions and recommendations.
- The objective of a review is to provide an unbiased assessment of the reviewed item, highlighting its strengths and weaknesses, and offering recommendations or insights to help readers make informed decisions.

STYLE AND ATTITUDE:

- Reviews adopt a balanced and informative tone, presenting both positive and negative aspects of the reviewed item in a fair and objective manner.
- The style is engaging and descriptive, providing detailed observations, analysis, and opinions to support the reviewer's assessment.
- Allows for personal anecdotes, experiences, or comparisons to enhance the review's relevance and relatability to the audience.

STANDARDS:

- Follows a structured format with an introduction providing context for the review, body sections discussing various aspects of the reviewed item, and a conclusion summarizing key points and offering final thoughts or recommendations.
- Presents information in a clear, organized manner, using specific examples, comparisons, or evidence to support the reviewer's opinions and conclusions.
- Considers the target audience and their interests, preferences,

and expectations when crafting the review, ensuring relevance and usefulness.

TIPS AND TEMPLATES:

Writing an effective review requires careful observation, analysis, and expression of opinions and recommendations. Tailor your review to the interests and expectations of the audience, providing relevant information and insights to help them make informed decisions.

- Present a balanced assessment of the reviewed item, acknowledging both its strengths and weaknesses. Avoid bias or personal preferences, focusing on objective observations and evaluations.
- Use vivid and descriptive language to bring the reviewed item to life for the reader, providing detailed descriptions, observations, and impressions. Engage the reader's senses and emotions to enhance their understanding and appreciation.
- **Useful Vocabulary:** Incorporate words and phrases that convey clarity, specificity, and relevance in describing and evaluating the reviewed item. Examples include "impressive," "flawless," "underwhelming," "innovative," "user-friendly," etc.
- **Idiomatic Expressions:** Use idiomatic expressions to add color and flair to your review, making it more engaging and memorable for the reader. Examples include "hit the nail on the head," "the bottom line," "a mixed bag," "take it with a grain of salt," etc.

IT'S ALWRITE!

REVIEW TITLE

Date:
Reviewers Name | Reviewers Title

Publication Name

Introduction:

Provide background information or context for the review

State the purpose or objective of the review

Body Sections:

Overview:

•Brief summary or introduction to the reviewed item

Features/Aspects:

Discuss various features, aspects, or elements of the reviewed item
Provide observations, analysis, and opinions on each aspect

Pros and Cons:

Highlight the strengths and weaknesses of the reviewed item

Offer comparisons or contrasts with similar items or alternatives

Conclusion:

Summarize key points and observations from the review

Offer final thoughts, recommendations, or ratings

Review Template

REVIEWS

EXAMPLE REVIEW

Burger Heaven: A Culinary Delight or Just Another Burger Joint?

Foodies Unite
Date: May 25, 2023
Reviewer: John Davis
Position: Food Critic
john.davis@foodcriticreviews.com

In the competitive world of fast food, standing out can be a tough challenge. Burger Heaven, a new entrant in the burger chain market, promises a heavenly dining experience with its gourmet burgers. This review evaluates whether Burger Heaven lives up to its name and hype, focusing on its menu, quality, service, and overall dining experience.

Burger Heaven recently opened its doors with a mission to elevate the classic burger experience. The chain boasts a menu filled with creative options, premium ingredients, and a modern, inviting ambiance. Their variety is impressive, featuring traditional beef burgers, chicken sandwiches, and vegetarian choices. Specialties like the "Heavenly Bliss Burger" and "Spicy Inferno" immediately caught my attention.

The emphasis on fresh, high-quality ingredients is evident in every bite. The beef is 100% Angus, and the buns are baked in-house daily. The vegetables were crisp and fresh, adding a nice balance to the hearty burgers. The "Heavenly Bliss Burger" was a delight, with a juicy patty, perfectly melted cheese, and a flavorful aioli sauce. The combination of flavors was well-balanced, making each bite a pleasure. However, take it with a grain of salt, as the "Spicy Inferno" was somewhat disappointing, with the spice overwhelming the other flavors.

One of the standout aspects of Burger Heaven is its ambiance. The interior is modern and clean, with comfortable seating and a casual, yet stylish atmosphere. It's a great place for a quick bite or a casual meal with friends and family. The staff at Burger Heaven were courteous and efficient, ensuring a pleasant dining experience. Orders were taken promptly, and the food arrived hot and fresh.

However, the gourmet touch comes with a higher price tag compared to other fast food chains, which might not appeal to all customers. Additionally, there was some inconsistency in the menu items, as demonstrated by the overpowering spice in the "Spicy Inferno."

Overall, Burger Heaven offers a promising take on the classic burger joint with its focus on quality ingredients and a diverse menu. While there are some areas for improvement, particularly in flavor balance and pricing, it largely succeeds in delivering a satisfying dining experience. I would recommend Burger Heaven to anyone looking for a gourmet burger experience. With a few tweaks, it has the potential to become a standout in the fast food industry.

Rating: 4 out of 5 stars.

Thank you for taking the time to read this review. I welcome your thoughts and comments on Burger Heaven or any other dining recommendations you might have. Feel free to share your opinions below or contact me by email.

PRACTICE TASKS:

Task 1: Film Review

You have recently watched a new release film that has been generating a lot of buzz. Write a review for a popular movie magazine that describes the plot, evaluates the performances of the actors, discusses the direction and cinematography, and gives your overall impression of the film. Be sure to provide a balanced view, highlighting both strengths and weaknesses.

Task 2: Hotel Resort Review

You recently stayed at a newly opened luxury resort during your vacation. Write a review for a travel website that details your experience. Describe the amenities, service quality, room comfort, dining options, and overall atmosphere of the resort. Include any notable positives and areas for improvement. Provide an honest evaluation to help future travelers decide whether to stay at the resort.

CHAPTER 16
SETS OF INSTRUCTIONS & GUIDELINES

A SET of Instructions and Guidelines is a comprehensive guide designed to help readers understand and complete a specific task or process efficiently and correctly. This text type is commonly used in various contexts, such as technical manuals, DIY projects, educational resources, and workplace procedures. The primary goal of instructions and guidelines is to provide clear, step-by-step directions that are easy to follow, ensuring that the reader can achieve the desired outcome with minimal confusion or errors.

Instructions and guidelines are typically written in a straightforward and concise manner, avoiding unnecessary jargon and complexity. They often include visual aids, such as diagrams, images, or charts, to enhance understanding and provide a visual representation of the steps involved. Effective instructions and guidelines are logically organized, starting with an introduction that outlines the purpose and scope of the task, followed by a detailed list of materials or tools required, and then the step-by-step instructions. Additionally, they may include troubleshooting tips, safety warnings, and additional resources for further assistance.

Writing a clear and effective set of instructions and guidelines requires attention to detail, thorough knowledge of the task or process, and the ability to anticipate and address potential challenges that the reader may encounter. The key is to make the instructions as user-friendly as possible, ensuring that readers of all skill levels can successfully complete the task.

SETTING, READERSHIP, OBJECTIVE

- Sets of instructions are detailed guides or procedures used to explain how to perform a task, operate a device, or complete a process.
- The readership of a set of instructions includes individuals who need guidance or assistance in performing the task or process described, ranging from novices to experienced users.
- The objective of a set of instructions is to provide clear, step-by-step guidance, enabling users to successfully complete the task or process with accuracy and efficiency.

STYLE AND ATTITUDE:

- Sets of instructions adopt a clear, concise, and straightforward style, using simple language and terminology to ensure understanding.
- The tone is instructional and informative, focusing on providing factual information and guidance rather than persuasion or entertainment.
- Allows for visual aids, diagrams, or illustrations to supplement written instructions and enhance clarity.

STANDARDS:

- Follows a structured format with a title or heading identifying the task or process, a list of materials or requirements needed, and step-by-step instructions organized in a logical sequence.
- Presents information in a sequential, chronological manner,

breaking down complex tasks into manageable steps and providing clear explanations and demonstrations.
- Uses numbered or bulleted lists, headings, and subheadings to organize information and facilitate navigation and comprehension.

TIPS AND TEMPLATES:

Writing clear and effective instructions requires careful consideration of the audience, task complexity, and potential pitfalls or challenges. Keep your instructions simple, specific, and easy to follow, providing clear explanations and demonstrations to guide users through each step.

- Use clear and precise language to convey instructions, avoiding ambiguity or confusion. Break down complex tasks into smaller steps and provide explicit details and explanations to ensure understanding.
- Incorporate visual aids, diagrams, or illustrations to complement written instructions and enhance clarity. Use arrows, labels, and annotations to highlight important details and demonstrate key steps or actions.
- Test your instructions with a sample audience or user group to identify any potential areas of confusion or misunderstanding. Revise and clarify instructions based on feedback to improve usability and effectiveness.
- Choose words and phrases that are familiar and easy to understand, avoiding technical jargon or unnecessary complexity. Examples include "assemble," "insert," "press," "rotate," "adjust," etc.

SETS OF INSTRUCTIONS & GUIDELINES

TASK OR PROCESS TITLE

Materials/Requirements:
List of materials, tools, or equipment needed to perform the task

Introduction:
Brief overview or introduction to the task or process

Explain the purpose or objective of the instructions

Step by Step Instructions:
Step 1:
Detailed instructions for the first step

Include any necessary preparatory actions or precautions

Step 2:
Detailed instructions for the second step

Provide clear explanations and demonstrations as needed

Step 3:
Detailed instructions for the third step

Ensure each step is clearly numbered or bulleted for easy reference

Include any troubleshooting tips or common pitfalls

Repeat Steps as Needed

Set of Instructions Template

EXAMPLE SET OF INSTRUCTIONS

How to Make a Perfect Cup of French Press Coffee

Materials/Requirements:

- French press
- Coffee beans
- Grinder
- Kettle
- Water
- Timer
- Stirring spoon
- Mug

Introduction:

Making a perfect cup of French press coffee is an art that combines the right technique and quality ingredients. This guide will help you brew a rich and flavorful cup of coffee using a French press, also known as a press pot or plunger pot. The objective of these instructions is to provide you with a step-by-step process to achieve a consistently delicious cup of coffee.

Step-by-Step Instructions:

Step 1: Measure and Grind the Coffee

- Measure out 1 ounce (about 28 grams) of coffee beans for every 17 ounces (about 500 milliliters) of water. Adjust the amount based on your taste preference.
- Grind the coffee beans to a coarse consistency, similar to sea salt. A consistent grind ensures even extraction and prevents over-extraction, which can lead to bitterness.

SETS OF INSTRUCTIONS & GUIDELINES

Step 2: Boil the Water

- Bring the water to a boil using a kettle. Once it reaches a boil, let it sit for about 30 seconds to cool slightly. The ideal water temperature for brewing French press coffee is around 200°F (93°C).
- Preheat the French press by filling it with hot water, then discard the water before adding the coffee grounds. This helps maintain the brewing temperature.

Step 3: Combine Coffee and Water

- Add the ground coffee to the preheated French press.
- Pour the hot water over the coffee grounds, making sure to saturate them evenly. Pour in a circular motion to ensure all grounds are wetted.
- Stir the mixture gently with a spoon to ensure all the coffee grounds are fully immersed in the water.

Step 4: Steep and Plunge

- Place the lid on the French press with the plunger pulled all the way up.
- Let the coffee steep for 4 minutes. Use a timer to ensure precise brewing time.
- After 4 minutes, slowly press the plunger down with steady pressure. Ensure you don't press too quickly to avoid forcing grounds through the filter.

Conclusion:

You've now made a perfect cup of French press coffee! Pour the brewed coffee into your mug and enjoy. Remember to clean your French press thoroughly after each use to maintain its performance and longevity.

Additional Tips/Resources:

- Experiment with different coffee-to-water ratios and steeping times to find your perfect brew.
- Use freshly roasted coffee beans for the best flavor.
- If the coffee tastes too bitter, try a coarser grind or shorter steeping time. If it's too weak, use a finer grind or longer steeping time.

By following these steps and tips, you'll be able to master the art of French press coffee and enjoy a rich, flavorful cup every time.

SETS OF INSTRUCTIONS & GUIDELINES

PRACTICE TASKS:

Task 1: Setting Up a Home Aquarium

Write a set of instructions for setting up a home aquarium. Your instructions should include a list of necessary materials, an introduction explaining the purpose of the instructions, detailed step-by-step instructions for setting up the aquarium, and any additional tips or resources.

Task 2: Activating a New School Email Account and Class Software

Create a set of guidelines for activating a new school email account and setting up the class software to help new students in your school. Include a list of required materials (e.g., computer, internet connection, activation codes), an introduction outlining the objective of the task, clear and detailed steps to activate the email account and install the class software, and a conclusion summarizing the process. Add any additional tips for troubleshooting or using the software effectively.

CHAPTER 17
SOCIAL MEDIA POSTS

SOCIAL MEDIA POSTS have become an integral part of our daily communication and online presence. These short, concise messages, often accompanied by visuals or multimedia, allow individuals to share their thoughts, experiences, and opinions with a potentially vast online audience. Social media posts come in various forms, from text-based updates and tweets to images, videos, and stories. They offer a platform for personal expression, connection with friends and followers, as well as engagement in discussions on a wide range of topics. In the context of education and communication, understanding the nuances of crafting effective and engaging social media posts is becoming increasingly important as these platforms continue to shape how we share information, interact, and express ourselves in the digital age.

SETTING, READERSHIP, OBJECTIVE:

- Social media/forum posts are brief messages or updates shared on online platforms such as Facebook, Twitter, Reddit, or discussion forums.
- The readership of a social media/forum post includes

SOCIAL MEDIA POSTS

- followers, friends, or members of the online community who engage with the platform.
- The objective of a social media/forum post varies depending on the context and platform but generally aims to inform, entertain, engage, or provoke discussion among the audience.

STYLE AND ATTITUDE:

- Social media/forum posts adopt an informal and conversational style, reflecting the tone and norms of the online community or platform.
- The tone is friendly, engaging, and relatable, encouraging interaction and participation from the audience.
- Allows for creativity, humor, or emotive language to capture attention and spark interest among users.

STANDARDS:

- Follows the conventions and limitations of the specific social media/forum platform, such as character limits, formatting options, and privacy settings.
- Presents information concisely and clearly, using hashtags, mentions, or links to enhance visibility and engagement.
- Encourages interaction and feedback from the audience through likes, comments, shares, or votes.

TIPS AND TEMPLATES:

Writing an effective social media/forum post requires understanding the platform's audience, culture, and features. Keep your post concise, engaging, and relevant to the interests of your followers or community members.

- Use questions, polls, or calls to action to encourage interaction

and participation from the audience. Prompt users to share their thoughts, experiences, or opinions on the topic.
- Incorporate images, videos, gifs, or emojis to enhance the appeal and visibility of your post. Visual content can help grab attention and convey emotions or messages more effectively than text alone.
- Use relevant hashtags and mentions to increase the discoverability of your post and connect with users who share similar interests or topics. Research trending hashtags or popular topics to leverage current conversations and trends.
- Consider the timing and frequency of your posts to maximize engagement and reach. Experiment with posting at different times of the day or week to identify when your audience is most active and receptive.
- A great text to use various idiomatic expressions and slang.

———

SOCIAL MEDIA POSTS

POST TITLE OR TOPIC

Date & Time of Posting:

Text Content:
Brief message or update sharing information, thoughts, or opinions

Keep the text concise, engaging, and relevant to the audience

Visual Content:
Insert image, video, gif, or emoji to complement the text

Use visual content to enhance the appeal and visibility of the post

Hashtags/Mentions:
Include relevant hashtags to increase discoverability

Mention individuals, brands, or communities to foster engagement

Call to Action:
Prompt users to like, comment, share, or engage with the post

Encourage interaction and participation from the audience

Social Media Post Template

EXAMPLE OF SOCIAL MEDIA POSTS

🚫 **Social Media Ban on Campus: Let's Talk!** 📱

Hey everyone, I wanted to share some thoughts on the recent ban our school implemented on using social media during school hours. For those who might not know, starting this week, the administration has prohibited all students from accessing social media platforms while on campus. They believe it will help us focus better on our studies and reduce distractions.

Personally, I have mixed feelings about this decision. On one hand, I understand the intention behind it. Social media can indeed be a significant distraction, and I've seen friends get sidetracked scrolling through feeds instead of paying attention in class. Plus, limiting our screen time could potentially lead to more face-to-face interactions, which is great.

However, I also think this ban is a bit extreme. Social media isn't just about memes and cat videos; it's a vital tool for communication and staying updated on important events. For instance, many school clubs and activities use social media to share updates and announcements. Completely cutting us off seems a bit harsh and might hinder these aspects of our school life.

I believe a more balanced approach would be better. Instead of a total ban, why not educate us on responsible social media use? Perhaps designated times for social media breaks could be allowed, ensuring we can still stay connected without it impacting our academic focus.

What do you all think? Let's discuss and see if we can find a middle ground that works for everyone! #SocialMediaBan #SchoolLife #Stay-Connected

SOCIAL MEDIA POSTS

PRACTICE TASKS:

Task 1: School Dress Code Changes

Your school recently introduced a new dress code policy that you feel strongly about. Write a social media post where you describe the details of what happened and explain whether you agree or disagree with the new policy. Share your thoughts and invite others to discuss their opinions.

Task 2: Banning Junk Food in School Cafeteria

Your school recently banned junk food in the cafeteria, replacing it with healthier options. Write a social media post where you describe the details of what happened and explain whether you agree or disagree with the new policy. Share your thoughts and invite others to share their perspectives on this change.

CHAPTER 18
SPEECHES

A SPEECH IS a formal or informal address delivered to an audience with the intent to inform, persuade, entertain, or inspire. Speeches are an essential form of communication used in various settings, including academic environments, professional meetings, public events, and personal occasions. The primary objective of a speech is to convey a message clearly and effectively, engaging the audience and leaving a lasting impression.

The structure of a speech typically includes an introduction, body, and conclusion. The introduction is designed to grab the audience's attention, introduce the topic, and establish the speaker's credibility. The body of the speech is where the main points are developed, supported by evidence, examples, and anecdotes. The conclusion summarizes the key points, reinforces the central message, and often includes a call to action or a memorable closing statement.

Speeches can vary in tone and style depending on their purpose and audience. They may be formal and serious, such as in a business presentation or academic lecture, or more casual and humorous, such as in a wedding toast or motivational talk. Effective speeches make use of rhetorical devices, storytelling, and emotional appeals to connect with the audience and enhance the impact of the message.

SPEECHES

Preparing and delivering a speech involves careful planning, practice, and attention to the audience's needs and expectations. Successful speakers not only focus on the content of their speech but also on their delivery, using body language, voice modulation, and eye contact to engage and persuade their listeners.

SETTING, AUDIENCE, OBJECTIVE:

- Speeches, presentations or openings of debates are formal presentations delivered to an audience in various settings such as conferences, meetings, or debates.
- The audience for a speech or opening of a debate includes attendees, participants, or stakeholders with an interest in the topic being addressed.
- The objective of a speech or opening of a debate is to present a compelling argument, provide context, and set the tone for the discussion or debate that follows.

STYLE AND TONE:

- Speeches or openings of debates adopt a formal and persuasive style, utilizing rhetorical devices and persuasive techniques to captivate the audience.
- The tone is confident, authoritative, and persuasive, aiming to establish credibility and command attention from the audience.
- Allows for emotional appeal, storytelling, or humor to engage the audience and make the speech memorable and impactful.

STRUCTURE AND CONTENT:

- Follows a structured format with an introduction, body, and conclusion, each serving a specific purpose in presenting the argument or setting the stage for the debate.
- The introduction provides background information on the

topic, establishes the speaker's credibility, and outlines the main points to be addressed.
- The body presents key arguments, evidence, and supporting points, organized logically to build a persuasive case and address potential counterarguments.
- The conclusion summarizes key points, reinforces the main argument, and leaves a lasting impression on the audience, inspiring action or further discussion.

TIPS AND TEMPLATES:

Delivering an effective speech or opening of a debate requires careful preparation, rehearsal, and consideration of the audience's interests and perspectives. Tailor your speech to resonate with the audience, capture their attention, and persuade them to consider your viewpoint.

- Organize your speech in a clear and logical manner, using transitions and signposts to guide the audience through the main points. Keep sentences and paragraphs concise and focused to maintain the audience's attention.
- Use rhetorical devices, such as repetition, analogy, or vivid imagery, to enhance the persuasive impact of your speech. Appeal to the audience's emotions, values, and beliefs to make your argument more compelling and memorable.
- Involve the audience in your speech by asking rhetorical questions, eliciting nods or gestures, or encouraging participation through interactive elements such as polls or Q&A sessions.
- Pay attention to your delivery style, including voice tone, pace, and gestures, to convey confidence and authority. Practice your speech multiple times to ensure fluency and coherence, and consider the timing constraints of the event or debate.
- **Useful Vocabulary:** Incorporate words and phrases that convey authority, clarity, and persuasiveness in your speech. Examples include "advocate," "underscore," "underscore," "underscore," etc.

SPEECHES

- **Idiomatic Expressions:** Use idiomatic expressions to add color and impact to your speech, making it more memorable and engaging for the audience. Examples include "hit the nail on the head," "food for thought," "call to action," "break the ice," etc.

OPENING STATEMENT/TITLE

Date & Location of Speech:

Introduction:

Greet the audience and establish rapport

Provide background information on the topic

State the purpose or objective of the speech

Body:
Main Point 1:

Present the first argument or perspective

Support with evidence, examples, or data

Main Point 2:

Present the second argument or perspective

Support with evidence, examples, or data

Main Point 3:

Present the third argument or perspective

Support with evidence, examples, or data

Speech Template

SPEECHES

EXAMPLE SPEECH

Introducing a School Recycling Program

May 12, 2024, Student Council Meeting Room

Good afternoon, esteemed members of the student council. Thank you for giving me the opportunity to speak today. My name is Alex Martinez, and I'm here to discuss an initiative that I believe can make a significant positive impact on our school community: the introduction of a comprehensive recycling program. As we all know, our environment is facing numerous challenges, and as students, we have a responsibility to take action. The purpose of my speech is to outline the benefits of a recycling program, provide a plan for implementation, and highlight how this initiative can enhance our school's sustainability efforts.

First and foremost, a recycling program will significantly reduce the amount of waste our school sends to landfills. Currently, our school generates a considerable amount of waste daily, much of which could be recycled. According to recent studies, schools can reduce their waste by up to 50% by implementing effective recycling programs. By separating recyclables such as paper, plastic, and metal, we can drastically cut down on the waste that contributes to environmental pollution. For example, recycling paper saves trees, water, and energy, which in turn helps combat deforestation and climate change.

Secondly, introducing a recycling program will educate and empower students to become more environmentally conscious. Education is a powerful tool, and by incorporating recycling into our daily routines, we can foster a culture of sustainability among students. This program can be integrated into the curriculum through projects and activities that teach the importance of recycling and its impact on the environment. For instance, we could organize workshops and invite guest speakers to discuss the benefits of recycling and share practical tips. This hands-on learning approach will not only increase awareness but also encourage students to adopt eco-friendly habits beyond the school environment.

Lastly, a recycling program can enhance our school's reputation as a leader in sustainability. In today's world, institutions that prioritize environmental responsibility are highly regarded. By implementing a successful recycling initiative, we can set an example for other schools and the broader community. This program can also open up opportunities for partnerships with local environmental organizations and businesses, further solidifying our commitment to sustainability. Imagine our school being recognized for its green initiatives, attracting more students, and fostering a sense of pride among current students and staff.

In summary, a school recycling program offers numerous benefits, from reducing waste and educating students to enhancing our school's reputation. I urge the student council to consider this proposal seriously and take the necessary steps to implement it. Together, we can make a difference and contribute to a healthier planet. As the saying goes, "We do not inherit the Earth from our ancestors; we borrow it from our children." Let's take this opportunity to leave a positive legacy for future generations. Thank you.

SPEECHES

PRACTICE TASKS:

Task 1: Implementing a New School Club

You have an idea to start a new school club focused on community service and volunteer work. Prepare a speech to present to the student council where you describe the details of the club, its benefits to the school and community, and how it can be implemented. Make sure to engage your audience and persuade them to support your proposal.

Task 2: Extending Library Hours

You believe that extending the school library hours will greatly benefit students, especially during exam periods. Write a speech to deliver to the school administration, explaining the reasons for extending library hours, the benefits it would bring to students' academic performance, and how the school can manage the extended hours. Use evidence and examples to support your argument and conclude with a compelling call to action.

ABOUT THE AUTHOR

MATT FLETCHER

Originally from the U.K., Matt Fletcher has taught internationally for over ten years, enriching his educational methods with diverse cultural insights. With extensive experience in both education and leadership, he excels at mentoring, coaching, and motivating students and professionals alike. Committed to promoting inclusive and collaborative atmospheres, Matt is passionate about creating learning environments that foster curiosity and providing resources that enable both teachers and students to excel and thrive.

You can connect with Matt via his website at matttfletcher.com or follow him on social media.

- instagram.com/matttfletcher
- linkedin.com/in/matttfletcher
- threads.net/@matttfletcher

www.ingramcontent.com/pod-product-compliance
Lightning Source LLC
Chambersburg PA
CBHW070429010526
44118CB00014B/1966